WOW
STORIES

Volume 1

Nina Stellwagen

Isaiah 41:10

NINA STELLWAGEN

WOW STORIES

**60 inspiring stories that demonstrate
the amazing love and power of God!**

Volume 1

HISproject

WOW STORIES
60 inspiring stories that demonstrate the amazing love and power of God
HISproject

Stories compiled and written by Nina Stellwagen
Edited by Diane G. H. Kilmer

Cover design by Kim Warner and Melody McNeill
Photo enhancing by Melody McNeill (www.mmmediadesign.com)
Cover photograph taken by Nina Stellwagen
Photo of author taken by Noelle Shaw

Book design by Christina Wert (www.sunlitnook.com)
Text type was set in Trebuchet MS

Unless otherwise identified, Scripture quotations are taken from the HOLY BIBLE, NEW INTERNATIONAL VERSION®, Copyright © 1973, 1978, 1984 International Bible Society. Used by permission of Zondervan. All rights reserved. Scripture quotations marked NKJV are taken from the New King James Version. Copyright © 1982 by Thomas Nelson, Inc. Used by permission. All rights reserved. Scripture quotations marked KJV are taken from the King James Version. All emphasis within Scripture quotations is the author's own. Please note the author of this book capitalizes all pronouns in Scripture and other content herein that refer to the Father, Son and Holy Spirit. The author chose not to capitalize the name of satan and related names with the result of violating some grammatical rules.

Quotes from: Marshall, Catherine, A Man Called Peter, Revell, a division of Baker Publishing Group, © 1951. Used by permission.

HISWOWSTORIES website design by Melody McNeill (www.mmmediadesign.com)
Website technical support by Andrew Jensen (ajens999@gmail.com)

ISBN-13: 978-1492348979

WOW STORIES is available at Amazon.com, also on Kindle

Call your local bookstore to order WOW STORIES; published by CreateSpace

This book is dedicated to:
My husband, Eric, whom I deeply love and respect. I
appreciate how he is always there for me.

My parents, Bob and Dolly Straley, who have lived 68 years of
marriage (and counting) dedicated to God, His service, to each
other and family. I am eternally grateful that God blessed me
with such loving and wonderful parents who taught me about the
Lord from my earliest childhood.

My children, Nicole, Noelle, Scott, Leah, John and James, who
are more precious and dear to my heart than words can express.

CONTENTS

Acknowledgments

Introduction

Fly Away Checks | 1
Miracle in the Storm | 4
You'll Never Smoke Again | 8
The Warning | 12
Clothesline Miracle | 15
I Read My Own Obituary | 18
Call Lori | 24
Tornado Warning | 26
I've Got Something to Tell You | 28
Turning Point | 31
Witch on the Run | 34
The Puppy | 37
Marry Jerry | 40
The Birthday Present | 44
Catherine's Comfort | 45
Lost Book | 49
Hip Hip Hurray | 51
Sevenfold | 54
Get Up, Noelle | 56
Army Blankets | 57
Amazing Love | 60
Liver Transplant | 63
The Oak Tree | 71
The Race Car | 72
Holy -In- Filling | 75
The Baby Blue Jay | 78
Revealing X-Ray | 80
How Lovely | 83

Divine Rescue | 86

Peace in the Pain | 88

Boiling Oil | 95

The Earring | 97

Surprise Harvest | 100

Quick Answer to Prayer | 103

School of Faith | 105

It's Lunch Time | 108

Getting Into Hot Water | 110

Multi-Purpose Miracle | 114

In God's Hands | 118

Memory Loss Gone | 120

Turn and Run | 122

The Small Things | 125

Swollen Head | 127

It's Never Too Late | 129

Upside Down Truck | 133

The Final Blow | 135

Heavenly Back Surgery | 139

Go Buy Groceries | 143

When God Touched Me | 145

Bibles to China | 150

The Porthole | 154

Can You Hear the Angels Singing? | 156

Just in Time | 159

The Still Center of the Storm | 162

The Phone Call | 164

Divine Appointment | 166

At Heaven's Gate | 168

Tap on the Shoulder | 172

Glimpse of Heaven | 174

The Odometer | 180

WOW of the WOW Stories | 183

ACKNOWLEDGMENTS

First, I want to thank my Lord and Savior Jesus for allowing me to be part of such a wonderful adventure! Because of Him, regardless of what comes my way, I go to bed each night with a sweet peace in my heart. Every morning I wake up knowing He has given me a purpose for living.

I would like to express special gratitude to my husband Eric, who sacrificially gave his blessing for me to give up my job so I could pursue my dream of writing. I am so grateful for the loving, caring, generous husband he is.

After spending seven years collecting and writing stories, I feel tremendous gratitude toward the individuals who gave of their time to be involved in this project.

I would like to give a very special thanks to Diane G. H. Kilmer, who spent countless hours doing the final prayerful edit of all the WOW stories. Although Diane earns her living as a freelance writer and editor, God placed it in her heart to take on this huge task without charge. Diane's expertise and insight as a seasoned writer have been invaluable. I was especially intrigued that she changed certain words or phrases so they could be understood by other cultures—something that never occurred to me. Diane was an answer to prayer that far surpassed my expectations.

My sister, Marie Root, has also been a huge blessing in this process. I lost track of all the hours she spent listening to and critiquing WOW STORIES as I read them to her. She had a keen sense when something did not sound right. I didn't always share Marie's understanding, but she would patiently explain it to me until I finally got it. She was always right! Marie has encouraged me in many special ways. I love and appreciate my sis.

My son Scott has been a godsend. Being sensitive to hearing from the Lord, he has called time and again to encourage me with a scripture passage, prayer or special word, ministering to my heart precisely when I needed it! Scott demonstrates the love of God, and words are not adequate to express how much this means to me.

I want to thank three very special friends; Mary Ann Miller, Debby Washburn and Claudia Wood. These women of God have prayed numerous times for me and the WOW STORIES book. I have been blessed beyond measure by their encouragement and powerful prayers, and don't know what I would have done without them.

A special thanks to Randy Siedlecki, who was the first person I shared with about the concept of writing a Wow Stories book. Randy exuberantly shared my enthusiasm. Besides greatly encouraging me, she invested her time and talents to get the project started. I will always be grateful for all of Randy's efforts in getting the Wow Stories book underway.

I greatly appreciate everyone who has prayed for me during this long process. I have no doubt prayer has made a remarkable difference.

Lastly, I want to thank all the people who shared their personal WOW testimonies. Only God knows the full impact their stories will have on those who read them. I have no doubt many hearts will be touched.

— *Nina Stellwagen*

INTRODUCTION

If every skeptic in the world tried to convince me that the Bible was a book of fairy tales and that God did not exist—their arguments would not have the slightest influence on me because I have experienced the reality of God!

Incredible encounters with God have been taking place all over the world. When I think about the miracles and wonders that have happened to me and to others, I get excited! In the four decades that have followed my commitment to Jesus Christ, I have experienced numerous astounding answers to prayer, as well as four extraordinary healings that doctors could not explain or take credit for.

These supernatural occurrences are further evidence that the rest of what God has promised will take place. Spending eternity in a kingdom of great beauty where there is no longer any sin, death, disease, pain or sorrow, but only joy and endless pleasures in the presence of the Lord, may sound too wonderful and far-fetched to be true. But someone who has been instantly healed from a long-time painful malady understands beyond any doubt that God is real and the eternal home He has promised His followers will also be a reality one day!

WOW STORIES contains accounts from ordinary people who have experienced astonishing answers to prayer, divine rescues, provisions, healings and much more from an extraordinary God! Some testimonies may be viewed as bizarre coincidences, but most challenge or defy human explanation.

The Wow stories are from the young and the old, from recent happenings to decades-old. Some of the miracles and astounding answers to prayer that occurred in my own life are recorded in this book, as well as from family, friends and referrals.

These testaments will build your faith, put hope in your heart and reveal the power of prayer! You will gain new insight into the tremendous depths of God's love, mercy and personal care for each of His children.

In the Bible, Psalm 96:3 tells us to, "Declare His glory among the nations, His marvelous deeds among all peoples." The intent of this book is to do just that!

—Nina Stellwagen

*He performs
wonders
that cannot be
fathomed,
miracles
that cannot be
counted.*

✤ Job 5:9 ✤

FLY AWAY CHECKS

NOTE FROM THE EDITOR: When I first began to collect stories for this book, a curious incident that happened to a businessman in Florida popped into my mind:

He was a young man who revered God and had recently started his own insurance agency. He had a habit of keeping several pages of company checks and a few other important papers in a three-ring binder. Whenever he left the office, he would take the notebook with him.

One day when leaving the agency, the man set the notebook on top of his car. After a few distractions, he climbed into his vehicle and drove off. Soon several people began honking their horns at him. Looking in his rearview mirror he saw papers flying everywhere and knew immediately what happened.

Quickly the man pulled over, jumped out of his car and raced around gathering up the papers and pages of checks that were blowing all over the busy streets of Fort Myers. When he could find

1

no more papers, he took inventory. Everything that had been in the notebook was recovered—except for one page of checks.

Later, the young businessman received a phone call from his surprised bookkeeper. His missing page of checks had blown through the business district, into the suburbs and then landed on her back doorstep! Teasingly, she told him it was a good thing the page of checks were by the back door, because they never used the front door and probably wouldn't have noticed it.

This event occurred more than thirty years ago when I lived Florida, so it did not seem feasible to get the story. But I liked the story's message: when we commit our lives to God, He often demonstrates His care in extraordinary and sometimes even humorous ways.

Deciding to pray about it, my prayer went something like: "Dear Lord, I really liked that story. Please give me another one just like it. In Your awesome sovereignty that would be a piece of cake for You."

A few weeks after saying that prayer, my husband Eric and I, along with the rest of my siblings, went on an Alaskan cruise to celebrate my parents' 60th wedding anniversary. During this vacation, my brother David and I got into a discussion about the then pending *WOW Stories* book and soon began telling each other amazing stories. When I told David the story about the fly away checks, he got a huge smile on his face and said, "Do you want to hear something really weird? The same thing happened to me!" David proceeded to tell his story:

"My friend Tony and I had recently started a copy machine repair business in Fort Myers. In the early days of the business, we kept important receipts, papers and usually about 15 pages of company checks in a three-ring binder. Every time I left the office, I took the binder with me.

"One day when leaving our building, I set the binder on top of my van while loading up a few things—then, in a hurry, drove off.

Soon I was on Cleveland Avenue when I noticed several people honking their horns at me. In my rearview mirror, I could see papers flying all over. Instantly I knew what happened, pulled over, jumped out of my vehicle and ran around picking up the pages of checks and papers. When it was all said and done, I could account for everything that had been in the notebook—except for one page of checks.

A couple hours later, I received a phone call.

"'Are you missing anything?' It was my insurance agent. He said he was driving down the road when a piece of paper slapped onto his windshield, then got stuck under one of his wiper blades. When he finally had a chance to pull over and remove the piece of paper—it was my missing page of checks!"

Wow! I'm convinced God orchestrated those two events just to put smiles on our faces.

By the way—did I mention that my brother's page of checks landed on the windshield of the businessman in the first story?!

"To Him who is able to do immeasurably more than all we ask or imagine, according to His power that is at work within us."

- Ephesians 3:20

—Nina Stellwagen, Michigan

MIRACLE IN THE STORM

On Memorial Day in 1978, my husband Dan and I, along with friends from church, Rick and Deanna—planned to spend the day sailing and fishing in the Florida Keys on their 26-foot Erwin sailboat. Leaving our three daughters and Rick and Deanna's son with a sitter, the four of us set sail that morning.

The weather was pleasant with a good breeze and not too hot. Once out of the bay, we put up the sails and headed for open water. On our way to investigate another bay, we noticed a foreboding black line on the horizon. Dan and Rick decided to turn the boat around and head back to the marina in Key Largo. Even with the kicker motor engaged and sails up, our top speed was still no match for the rapidly approaching storm. As we approached the marina, the storm overtook us.

The rain came down so hard we could no longer see where we were going. Gusts of wind moved the boat towards shore. Everything became chaotic and the boat could no longer hold direction. Dan and Rick quickly took the sails down. Knowing other boats had anchored to wait out the storm, they became concerned we might ram someone and decided to anchor down where we were. Several attempts were made before the anchor seemed to catch securely. The guys were drenched when they finally came below deck where Deanna and I were huddled together in the cabin.

Dan checked the depth finder, which revealed we were in five feet of water. We thought we were in a safe location, but just then, Dan looked out the window and saw a shadow approaching us. The anchor had not held, and we were drifting toward a cluster of trees in the mangroves! The guys scrambled up on deck. Dan planned to pull up the anchor while Rick got the motor going and put the boat in reverse to move us away from the trees.

Then the real nightmare began! The wind whipped the front of the boat around and the mast hit some high-tension power lines. The main power line snapped and hit the anchor Dan was pulling in!

Dan's body was instantly seized into a fetal position, and his arms clamped to his chest as the electrical jolt hurled him from the boat.

The electrical charge set off a series of violent explosions that went through the wiring on the boat, melting halyards and exiting the fiberglass boat from many places. Below deck where Deanna and I were sitting, the whole inside of the cabin seemed to explode! Thinking lightning had struck us, we ran up on deck through smoke and burning objects.

Realizing the boat was sinking, Rick yelled, "Get off the boat now!" He hoped I would not see or have time to realize what had happened to Dan. At the time, I thought Dan must have already jumped off the front of the boat and was safe. When I asked Rick about Dan he didn't answer, but I assumed he was preoccupied with trying to get Deanna and me safely away from the boat.

The water we were in was only about four to five feet deep, but the bottom was made up of thick oozing mud. Rick began leading us women away from the boat, when Dan emerged near the bow of the boat, gasping for breath, coughing and in obvious distress. Rick was stunned. He had witnessed Dan being forcefully thrown from the boat and was sure he was dead. Greatly relieved, Rick made his way over to aid Dan.

Soon we all joined hands and started walking together toward the shore, fearful that electrocution might still be a threat. With strong winds blowing and our trudging through silt and mud, and water up to our necks—it seemed hopeless that we would ever reach the shore. I thought, *This is impossible. We'll never make it.*

At last, the water became shallower. Even though the rain was still pouring, we could finally see the shore. We looked back to see the sunken boat listing at 45 degrees. Although we were completely exausted, our lives had been spared!

The magnitude of our miracle was unknown to us until later, when we learned that the power line our boat hit was the main feeder line for Key West and carried more than 100,000 volts! Due to our boating accident, power was shut off to the entire Florida Keys.

Those who saw the charred remains of our sunken sailboat could not believe that everyone on our boat had survived. Assuming loss of life had occurred, a Coast Guard vessel arrived an hour after the accident to collect the bodies.

In every area of this experience, we could see the hand of God. Remarkably, not one of us suffered any injuries when the sailboat's mast hit the power line. The high voltage set off explosions that blasted pieces of molten halyards throughout the vessel, instantly melting through the boat's fiberglass body. Rick was operating the motor when the electrical charge went through it, leaving a hole the size of a silver dollar. A melted cable dropped onto the handle of the motor just inches from Rick's hand. We later counted more than thirty holes in the boat, many of them large enough to put a fist through. Several of the holes were below deck in the cabin where Deanna and I were when everything began exploding! Multiple holes below the boat's water line caused it to sink quickly. Our radio, depth finder and all electronic equipment were burned and completely destroyed.

Incredibly, Dan did not sustain any burns from the immense electrical current that went through his body. Even more astonishing, Dan never lost consciousness! As he lay face down in the water, unable to move with his legs cramped and drawn up behind him, Dan believed he was dying. He remembers thinking, *Who would have thought this was the way I am going to die?* But a deep calm settled over him and he was ready to meet his God. Yet, soon after, Dan regained the use of his legs!

The accident had been on the news and initally reported there were no survivors. Our babysitter'sparents were watching the news when it was first reported. Although names were not being given, they recognized Rick's boat. Fearing the worst, they called their daughter so she would be prepared to stay with the children until "details could be worked out. Our oldest daughter, who was nine, overheard the conversation and thought she and her sisters were orphans.

Following the ordeal, Dan went in for a thorough medical checkup and was given a clean bill of health by his amazed doctor. From time to time when Dan ponders his experience, he realizes there is no way he should have survived—yet, to this day he has not had one health problem related to that accident. God is so good!

God was in our boat that day. We were protected through every inch of our nightmarish experience. We were benefactors of a series of extraordinary miracles brought on by a very personal, loving God. We still experience His pleasure in the retelling of this story.

—Joy & Dan Straley, Colorado

YOU'LL NEVER SMOKE AGAIN

For much of my adult life I was hopelessly addicted to smoking cigarettes. I smoked my first cigarette around the age of 14 to be part of the in-crowd at school. Once I moved out on my own, smoking became intertwined with every aspect of my life.

Smoking was my incentive to crawl out of bed in the morning. I smoked while planning my day and to reward myself every time I accomplished something. Somehow, I felt like I could think and communicate better with a cigarette in my hand. Cigarettes were my motivation to press on in daily life and my comfort when I was upset. Except when I was sleeping, at work, or attending events where smoking was prohibited, I rarely went more than 15 minutes without having a cigarette.

With all the publicity about the hazards of smoking, I finally decided to quit. To my dismay, trying to live my life without cigarettes left me completely distraught. As a Christian, I believed in God, read my Bible and prayed daily. However, this was an area of my life where I seemed to have no control.

In my early forties I was still smoking. My 25-plus years of this nasty habit began to take its toll. In the mornings, I began wheezing and having difficulty breathing. My lungs developed a stinging sensation and it actually became physically uncomfortable to smoke at times. I also began coughing up what looked like rusty red fisheggs several times a day, leaving me with the dismal concern that I was likely on the brink of getting lung cancer or emphysema. Adding to my despair was the thought that my secondhand smoke could be harming my children and husband.

More than anything else, I wanted smoking out of my life and made numerous determined attempts to quit. Each time I would tear up my cigarettes—but within hours, I would begin to sink into a dismal depression and was barely able to function. Not only did I neglect my household duties, but those around me were subjected to my despair and anger. Usually within 36 hours, I was desperately searching for a cigarette in the trash that I could tape back together to smoke on the way the nearest store to get another pack.

The time came when I assessed all my attempts to quit smoking as a time of torture, followed by inevitable failure.

Feeling sure that God was totally disappointed in me and upset with me, I felt guilty most of the time. I had to face the truth; smoking was a merciless hindrance in my life that was on the verge of killing me, and I seemed powerless to overcome it. I felt like the biggest failure in the world.

Out of desperation, I began to cry out to God about my addiction. Every time I lit up a cigarette I would say a prayer, something on the order of: "Dear God, I'm so sorry! Please help me! I hate this, but I can't seem to quit! I want to do what pleases You! I'm sorry I fail—I don't want to! I want smoking out of my life! Please help me!"

One day I was sitting outside smoking a cigarette, pouring my heart out to God as usual—when suddenly, God clearly spoke to me and said, "I love you even though you smoke, and I'm going to deliver you soon!" A sweet peace came over me—it almost felt as though someone poured warm oil over me! I sat there stunned for several minutes.

For the first time in years, I was not feeling any guilt. I could hardly believe God said He loved me, even though I smoked. I had been so sure He was disappointed with me and probably even angry about my smoking. Somehow, I became aware that God loved me deeply in-spite of my smoking. He no longer seemed like a God with a billy club, ready to clobber me, but like Someone who was filled with compassion for me—my best interest was the object of His heart!

About three weeks later on February 22, 1993, while standing in my kitchen, I took my pack of cigarettes off the top of the refrigerator. After pulling a cigarette out, I had it up to my mouth ready to light, when God spoke to me again, saying, "Now is the time of your deliverance—you will never smoke again."

Instantly I felt like someone who had never smoked before!

The cigarette in my hand now felt like a foreign object. I stood there in awe, marveling over what was happening. There was no need to tear up my remaining cigarettes—I simply threw them, carton and all, into the trash.

About a week later, my "smoking buddies" were coming over, and I could not help but wonder how this was going to work out. The normal procedure for us girls was to smoke almost nonstop while we drank coffee or pop and visited.

When the girls came over I told them about my miracle. They too were astounded. I'm sure they felt a little uncomfortable that I was not smoking with them, but I could only silently continue to marvel that I truly had no interest or desire to smoke.

The entire time the girls were at my house, God performed another wonder. As we sat in the kitchen, their cigarette smoke swirled all around me, but I could not smell it! Thinking something might be wrong with my nose, I got up and smelled a scented candle that was on a nearby counter. The apple-cinnamon aroma was distinct, and I knew my nose was working just fine.

As days, then weeks rolled by, I never experienced withdrawals, cravings or sense of emotional loss—nor has it ever bothered me to be around others who smoke. God did a tremendous miracle in my life, and I could not take one speck of credit for it!

Twenty years have passed since God miraculously delivered me from smoking.

Although it took nearly two years for my lungs to clear up, I am in good health now and feel great, thanks be to God! I have no doubt that if God had not answered my cry for help, I would still be smoking—if I were still alive.

How wonderful it is that God hears the cry of our hearts! God never ceased to love me while I was still imprisoned by my addiction. He just wanted me to be free! How comforting are His promises:

"The LORD is a refuge for the oppressed, a stronghold in times of trouble. Those who know Your name will trust in You, for You, LORD, have never forsaken those who seek You."

- Psalm 9:9-10

—Anonymous, Michigan

THE WARNING

At age 20, I was still living at home, attending college and working a part-time job. I did not have a car so I would often take the city bus to get to and from school and my job.

Although I had grown up in a Christian home and believed there was a God, I had only recently truly dedicated my life to Him. God went from being my parents' God to being my best friend. Instead of thinking all the old thoughts that used to fill my mind, I began to spend most of my time thinking about God and talking to Him. I would tell Him how much I loved Him, sing praises to Him, and pray in my prayer language (1 Corinthians 14:2). God began filling me with much-needed peace.

One morning while riding the bus home after school, I was talking to God and praying in my prayer language when suddenly an audible voice spoke to me and said, "Something's going to happen to you today."

Startled, I looked around to see who was talking to me. To my surprise, the seats all around me were empty; a few passengers sat at the front of the bus. Feeling just a tinge of fear, I continued praying.

A few minutes later that same voice spoke again, repeating the same message: "Something's going to happen to you today."

This time a big smile came over my face. The trace of fear completely left and, instead, I began to feel overjoyed as I realized it was the Lord who had spoken to me. Feeling totally calm, I asked Him, "What Lord? What's going to happen to me?"

He spoke again, "Something's going to happen to you today, but you're going to be OK." Feeling a sweet calm, I continued to pray, but numerous times my curiosity got the best of me and I would ask, "Lord, what's going to happen to me?"

I was reassured with His words, "You're going to be OK." My joy kept growing until I thought my heart would burst!

After I arrived home, I felt curious all day about what was going to happen to me. The day went by quickly and soon I was back on the city bus, heading for the evening shift at the sub shop where I worked.

During my ride, I again asked the Lord what was going to happen to me. This time I began to hear over and over in my mind, "I have not given you a spirit of fear, but of power, love and a sound mind"—words based on a precious Bible verse (2 Timothy 1:7, NKJV). It was just what I needed to hear.

Throughout the evening, while my coworker prepared sandwiches and I worked at the cash register, I wondered what would happen. When business became unusually slow, the girl working with me went to the back room to start cleaning and preparing for the next day.

A short time later, a very solemn-looking young man walked in, appearing to be in his early 20s. I welcomed him to our store with the usual greeting and a warm smile. The grim-looking man never made eye contact, nor attempted a reply, but nervously walked straight past me and down the hall to the restroom.

Immediately I knew this was it—the time had arrived for the "something" to happen to me. Not only did I feel calm, but also the joy of the Lord began to well up within me as I waited for the young man to come out of the bathroom. When he returned, he began nervously looking around. With a huge smile stuck on my face, I asked him if I could take his order. He mumbled something at me that I could not understand.

Then it happened! From under his jacket, he pulled out his hand that was covered with a paper bag, concealing whatever weapon he had, and then pointed it at my face!

Now realizing what he must have said, I quickly opened the cash register and began shoving the contents his way. The entire time I could not stop smiling! It all seemed so exciting and wonderful that God had totally prepared me ahead of time for this very moment.

The young man looked perplexed. He kept staring at me as if he thought I was crazy. Then—in a flash—he was out the door.

The girl who had been in the back room finally poked her head out the door and asked if someone was there. Still not able to wipe the smile off my face, I said, "Not anymore—we were robbed!"

She thought I was joking and said, "Nuh-uh! You're way too calm!" Then I opened the drawer to expose the empty cash register. Her jaw dropped! Without delay, we called the owner, who in turn called the police. The store was shut down for the night. The police arrived shortly, and I continued feeling happy and calm all during their questioning. They showed me mug shots of various men, but I was unable to identify any of them as the young man who robbed our store.

When it was all over, I lost my job. The owner thought my exuberantly happy and composed behavior was suspicious, leading him to believe I must have somehow been in on the crime, even though they could find no evidence to prove it. My dad was furious and offered to help me fight to get my job back, but it just did not seem necessary to me.

Pondering the situation later, I thought perhaps the other employee might have panicked resulting in her harm. Or maybe God was letting me learn that nothing is hidden from Him and we are always under His watchful care. Whatever His reasons, that memory will always put a smile on my face!

—Nicole Nolley, Florida

CLOTHESLINE MIRACLE

In 1953, my husband Bob and I lived in Rosebush, Michigan, where he pastored a small Methodist church between working fulltime at Central Michigan Community Hospital and attending Central Michigan University. I stayed home to care for our four children, the youngest still a baby.

Doing laundry in those days was not a simple task. Like many families, we had no indoor plumbing. To fill the washing machine, water was carried in by the pailful the night before. Then we put what was called a "hot water bug" into the machine, which was plugged into an electrical outlet. This would heat up the water overnight. Early in the morning we began washing clothes. The same water was used to wash everything, so the lightest colors and least-soiled things were washed first. After each load, every item was carefully fed through the wringer. Then everything went into a tub of rinse water and then fed through the wringer again.

After washing, we carried each load outside, shook the wrinkles out the best we could and then hung it all on the clothesline. Once dry, nearly everything needed to be ironed. Usually I had to do 10 to 12 loads of laundry, which was an all-day job.

After having a complete hysterectomy, I was unable to do laundry for several days. The kids, my husband and I desperately needed clean clothes to wear, and the baby's diapers were about to run out. When I finally felt well enough to tackle laundry the next day, we filled the washtub that evening and put in the hot water bug.

The following morning, as I looked out the window and saw the sky looking dark and overcast, my heart sank.

All my life while growing up, my mother instilled in us children a deep sense of faith and trust in God during hard times. Now, faced with a dilemma and not knowing what else to do, I said a simple prayer: "Lord, You know I need to get my laundry done. The kids need clothes and the baby needs diapers. Please make a way for me to get my clothes dry somehow!" In faith, I put the sheets in to wash. As soon as they were done, I put another load in to wash, then went directly outside and hung the sheets up to dry.

In the meantime, I sent our oldest son Dan down the street to give the rent money to our landlord. After Dan handed her the money, she asked him, "What's your mother doing?"

Dan told her, "She's washing clothes."

The landlady responded, "Well, she won't get them dried today. It's going to rain."

Dan replied, "Well, my mom's praying that God will let her clothes get dried somehow."

The landlady retorted, "Well, everyone else is praying it will rain, and we need it badly. The farmers' crops are burning up."

The sky was darkening rapidly and the landlady told Dan he had better get going. Before Dan arrived home it began to sprinkle. He was no sooner in the house when torrential rains began.

Looking out our front door, the rain was coming down so hard that I could barely see the end of our driveway, which was already beginning to flood. Every direction I looked the rains were pouring down, except, when I opened our back door, I could barely believe my eyes! To my astonishment, a dry area that resembled a wide hallway extended out to the clothesline to an area surrounding the clothesline of approximately 10 to 15 feet in every direction, which was also dry. This dry area resembled a large room bordered by walls that were sheets of rain coming down—a peculiar and amazing sight to behold!

The air in this "outdoor room" was extremely windy and the sheets I had recently hung on the line were flapping around wildly, already dry! As the day went on, the rains fluctuated from heavy to light, but never completely stopped. I hung up load after load of clothes, but not a drop of water touched the laundry or me. Due to the wind, everything dried in record time. By 3:00 p.m., I had hung out and dried over 10 bushels of laundry, while rain continued to pour all around me!

Later I learned that our county received nearly seven inches of rain that day, even causing flooding in some areas. That God had answered my prayer in such a miraculous way truly boosted and strengthened my faith. I realized that God cares about even the smallest details of our lives. He answered the prayer of a desperate mother to dry her laundry as well as the prayers of the distressed farmers for the rain they needed to save their crops. What a wonderful God we have!

—Dolly Straley, Florida

I READ MY OWN OBITUARY

My love for flying was born when I was 15 years old. My father had taken my two brothers and me to an air show in Battle Creek, Michigan. Watching those pilots put on a magnificent display of aerobatics completely enamored me; I was bitten by the "flying bug." Soon I started to dream about flying cars, buses, trucks and boats.

Through the years, my dreams of flying continued until, in the late 1980s, I decided to take flying lessons and got my solo license. Over the next couple years, I put in more than 200 flying hours through business trips taken all over South and Central Florida. I enjoyed every minute of it.

Eventually, two other men partnered with me to purchase a 1978 Piper Lance—a high-performance airplane with seating for six, retractable gear, auto pilot and air conditioning. This amazing plane was almost identical to the Saratoga in which John Kennedy, Jr. died. The only difference was that the Lance had a T-tail where the Saratoga had a straight tail. A great deal of my time was spent in this airplane, flying back and forth to our family vacation home in North Carolina and making numerous business trips all over Florida.

In the summer of 1996, I was flying to Fort Lauderdale for a convention and speaking engagement. Also aboard the Piper Lance was my wife, our two little girls—ages six and four—and our nanny, a 64-year-old Pentecostal Christian. They were all in the back of the plane, which had club seating, like a café booth with chairs on each side of a table. My set of golf clubs was in my co-captain seat. The trip was only 35 to 40 minutes and I was flying via visual flight rules. Our destination was the Fort Lauderdale Executive Airport.

My youngest daughter was always reluctant to fly and for the first time she wanted to talk to me with her mother's headset. We had just exchanged "I love yous" when I notified Miami center that I had my airport in sight and requested a frequency change to the local tower.

After being cleared to begin my descent, I turned off the auto pilot. Turning the plane to the right, I started a descent from my altitude of 3,000 feet. When descended to about 2,500 feet, the yoke started to push back at me and the nose of the airplane wanted to go up. This was the first time I had ever experienced this.

Quickly, I checked my trim wheel and it was all the way forward. All of a sudden, the stall horn blared and the plane went into a stall. Immediately, I began the recovery procedure, which meant getting the nose down so the airplane could regain enough speed to start flying again. A small plane loses approximately 300-500 feet in altitude when recovering from a stall. Looking out the window, I noticed we were over the Everglades near where the Value Jet had recently gone down.

The plane had no sooner recovered from the stall when my wife Marsha grabbed the headset from our daughter and said, "What the heck is going on? You're scaring the kids!"

Shaken, I told her, "It's scaring me, too! I don't know. Maybe we have a weight and balance issue."

Although our aircraft had recovered from the stall, the nose continued to want to go up. The only way to keep the nose of the plane down was to push on the yoke with every ounce of strength I had. Before long, my arms began to quiver from the pain. Maneuvering my body in the seat, I braced my knee on the yoke.

In an additional effort to get the nose of the plane to go down, I instructed everyone to get unbuckled from their seats and move as far forward in the cabin as possible. Just as they all had moved, we went into another stall. As the plane began to free-fall, Marsha, the kids and Nanny all became weightless, floating to the ceiling, only to be slammed back down when the plane recovered from the second stall.

After picking herself up from under the table, Marsha immediately grabbed her headset and screamed at me to throw my golf clubs out the door. She was convinced they had thrown the plane's weight off.

Marsha had barely got everyone back in their seatbelts, when I felt a third stall was imminent. At this point, I was desperate and made a very critical error—I banked the plane very sharply to try and get the nose down. Banking the airplane while in a stall caused it to go into a fatal flat spin.

Having read the manual from front to back, I knew this airframe would not recover from a spin. In flight training we were warned several times to never practice spins with a Lance; they just do not recover. It was then I realized—we were all going to die.

At that moment, when the world was spinning 360 degrees, I saw a vision of my obituary and actually read the headline in our local paper, clearly and distinctly: *Longtime Insurance Agency owner dies in a small plane along with his wife, two children and their nanny.*

The hardest words I have ever uttered were on the tip of my tongue. Speaking into my headset, I asked Marsha if she was online. Immediately she replied, asking, "What is going on, Tim?!"

Responding with the painful truth, I told her, "I have lost control. We are in a spin and this plane will not come out of it. You need to say your prayers, hug the kids and I am so sorry, honey. We are not going to survive this. I love you!"

Marsha's reply is one I will never forget. She said, "That is totally unacceptable to me—do something and do it now!"

The way you recover from a spin in most planes is to release your grip on the yoke and hit the opposite rudder from the direction of the spin. As I attempted to apply this remedy again, it was no surprise that the plane would not respond.

So as we continued our spiral of death, I said my last prayers for my family and myself and asked God that it be painless for all of us. I remember asking God's forgiveness, being at peace with Him, and not being afraid to die. Knowing my innocent little girls, my wife and our nanny would also lose their lives—obviously due to my love of flying, certainly not theirs—filled me with guilt and sorrow. It seemed so unfair to them.

Frantically, I continued to stomp on the right rudder. The earth below was becoming eerily close. Impact was only moments away—when suddenly the plane came out of the spin! Totally shocked, I looked at the altimeter. We were 250 feet above the ground! My first reaction was, "Thank you, Jesus!"

With the stall horn still blaring, I noticed that with my knee on the yoke and the current power setting of the engine, we were actually flying again, although just under a stall. Below us was a four-lane highway, and all I wanted to do was get the plane on the ground.

Declaring an emergency with the air traffic controller at Executive Airport, I told her of my plan to put the plane down on the Sawgrass Expressway. She informed me it was rush hour and she doubted that there was any room to land the plane without causing great harm.

Then she asked if I could see Executive Airport—which was now five miles away at three o'clock—and asked if I thought we could make it that far. It didn't seem like we had a prayer to make it five miles at 250 feet above the ground, but I told her I would give it a try. My legs and arms were about to give out, and the stall horn continued blaring in my ears.

As we crossed over a community called Westin, I remember looking out the window and feeling as though I could just reach out and touch the roofs of those houses. If we stalled again, there would not be enough altitude for the plane to recover. We would simply crash into one of those homes.

When we were about one mile from the edge of the runway was the first time I actually thought that we might just make it back from the dead! The emergency crews had been activated. Once our plane was over the runway, I made a rather high nose, perfect landing.

The air traffic controller asked if we were all OK or if anyone needed medical attention. When I answered that we were all OK, she instructed me to slip onto the next taxiway between the runways, so that the planes on hold could get airborne, and those circling in the air, onto the ground.

We sat on the taxiway for 30 minutes. The fire trucks and rescue vehicles sat next to us with their lights rotating. Not one of us uttered a single word during that time. We were all in a state of shock. Miraculously, we had just been given a second chance at life.

Finally, we were cleared by the airport control center to taxi in. A friend was waiting to pick us up. He greeted us, joking that with the escort we had, he thought a celebrity had landed. But when he saw the look on our faces, he knew something was wrong.

Asking him to give me a couple minutes, I went directly to the men's room and lost my lunch. My doctor later told me it was due to all the adrenalin in my system.

During the entire ride to the hotel, I was unable to carry on a conversation. I asked my friend's indulgence to give me until dinner to explain what happened. Once in my room, I laid across the bed for 40 minutes, exhausted.

Marsha, who usually accompanied me to all the parties and meetings, did not come to a single one that weekend. She spent the entire time with the kids, counting her blessings and feeling it was a miracle to be alive.

The next day the head mechanic called to tell me that the pitch portion of the auto pilot did not disengage, which made the airplane want to be at 3,000 feet. He informed me that several fatal incidents are reported each year as results of runaway trim or malfunctioning auto pilot.

Only a few weeks earlier, he added, a local incident that killed a pilot and passenger had occurred, due to an auto pilot malfunction that was just the opposite of mine—the plane wanted to go down rather than up. The pilot was unable to control the airplane to a safe landing. The mechanic said he had never heard of anyone successfully fighting a pitch malfunction of the auto pilot all the way to a successful landing.

No one has ever been able to explain why our plane suddenly came out of the flat spin at 250 feet above the ground! At the onset of the plane's malfunctioning, our nanny—who was not wearing a headset and should not have been able to hear my voice over the noisy engine—said she heard me call out to God for help and began fervently praying as well.

My wife Marsha and I have never questioned that we had divine intervention that day. There is no doubt in our minds that God heard our prayers and performed a miracle; that one or all of our angels stopped our plane from spinning and held it in the sky long enough for us to get down safely!

Many pilots will tell you that flying is 99 percent boredom and one percent sheer terror. I've had my 1 percent. Although I still love to fly, I gave it up because I was alone in the air after that. My family will only fly commercial now. But I thank God for our survival!

—Tim Shaw, Florida

CALL LORI

One day I was sitting on the couch in my living room praying and talking to God, when all of a sudden He clearly spoke to me, saying, "Call Lori _____ and tell her I see her heart and tell her I love her."

The message startled me. I know three women named Lori very well. When God spoke to me, He said her first and last name, and then gave a clear-cut message of what He wanted me to say.

A mental battle immediately rose up inside me. Doubtful thoughts plagued my mind: *Was this just me? What if Lori isn't home? What if … ? What if … ?* I did not want to make the call. Yet, no matter how hard I tried, I could not get the message out of my mind, nor could I rid myself of the pressing feeling that God wanted me to call Lori.

Finally, I picked up the phone and dialed her number. When Lori answered, I decided just to blurt out what God had spoken to me:

"Lori, God told me to call you and tell you that He sees your heart and that He loves you." There was dead silence on the other end of the phone. I wondered if Lori hung up on me. Then I heard quiet sobbing in the background.

Once Lori was able to talk, she told me that she had been going through a very difficult trial. In her distress, she had cried out to God, saying, "Can You see my heart? Do You love me?" Now I was marveling at God's precise answer to Lori: "...tell her I see her heart and tell her I love her."

God's personal word to Lori was just what she needed to hear at that moment to strengthen and encourage her. Both of us were overjoyed, realizing God loves and cares for each of us more than we could ever imagine. ("The Lord is close to the brokenhearted and saves those who are crushed in spirit." Psalm 34:18)

But the story didn't end here.

When Lori went to work that night, she told a coworker named Chris about the personal Word God had given. Chris said to Lori, "I wish she would pray for me."

At the time, I did not know Chris or anything about her, but God's Word does tell us to pray for others. So I began praying for Chris. Shortly after my prayer began, the Lord spoke to me and said, "Tell Chris that her brother is with ... "

That stopped me dead in my tracks! I knew the Lord was going to finish the statement with the word "Me." I instantly panicked.

This implied Chris had a deceased brother. Uncertainties quickly entered my thoughts. *What if Chris doesn't have any brothers? Not to mention, a dead brother!* My faith plummeted as doubts and fears overtook me. My decision was made; neither Chris, nor Lori, would hear this risky Word from God.

A few weeks later Lori and I were talking when Chris came up in our conversation. Lori mentioned that Chris had been burdened about something for some time; her brother had been killed in a car accident and she was concerned as to whether or not he made it into heaven. Although he was raised in a Christian home, it appeared he had forsaken his childhood teachings. Often times he partied with his friends and was out drinking when he was killed.

Now, I admitted my fault to Lori. I told her about the earlier prayer and what God had spoken to me concerning Chris's brother. Lori, in turn, told Chris. Soon the entire family found out about "God's special Word" to Chris. They were all so happy!

These incidents taught me a good lesson about recognizing God's voice and being obedient—without dwelling on doubts. Thank goodness, God does not stop loving us when we falter—He just keeps teaching us!

Once again, I was reminded of how great God's love, mercy and compassion is towards us—far surpassing our human understanding!

"What is man that you are mindful of him, the son of man that you care for him? You made him a little lower than the angels; you crowned him with glory and honor and put everything under his feet."

- Hebrews 2:6-8

—Nina Stellwagen, Michigan

TORNADO WARNING

In 1957, my husband Carl and I were living in our very first home, four miles southwest of Sandusky, Michigan. My husband had purchased the previously damaged mobile home at a real bargain. Being a handyman, Carl did all the repair work himself. His parents let us put the trailer behind their house.

One summer afternoon Carl had just arrived home from work. He sat down on the couch in the living room and started playing with our 18-month-old son. Our six-week-old baby girl was sleeping on a bed in the back of the trailer, and I was in the kitchen making spaghetti sauce. It was a beautiful sunny day. Music was playing on the radio and everything seemed perfect—until, while stirring the spaghetti sauce, I suddenly had an overwhelming urge to go look out the door on the south side of the trailer.

It felt like I had no choice in the matter. God seemed to take hold of me and steer me right over to the door. Looking out, I noticed big, rolling, black clouds behind my in-laws' house that looked like billows of smoke rising to the air from a huge bonfire.

Suddenly the wind picked up. Alarmed, I said to Carl, "We've got an awful storm coming. Let's get to the house!" Frantically, I began praying: "Lord, I don't know what's coming at us, but please put Your arms around us. We need You!" My husband picked up our son while I ran to the back of the trailer and grabbed the baby, quickly wrapping her up in a blanket. We ran to the door but could not open it; the wind had sealed us in.

My husband, a big, strong man, somehow managed to get the door open. But no sooner had we made it down the steps than the wind threw us to the ground. Unable to stand up, we were only a few feet away from the trailer when it was lifted off its foundation by powerful, swirling winds. For a brief moment, we could see completely underneath it, and then watched as our mobile home was flipped away from us, landing on its side.

We began crawling on our hands and knees toward my in-laws'

house—every inch a struggle. The wind was so forceful that our eyelids seemed to be blown shut, and we could barely see. The baby was clutched in my arms when the wind sucked away the blanket she was wrapped in, sending it whirling up into the air. I was not even sure she was still in my arms, but I kept holding tightly.

From a row of tall pine trees next to our driveway, two trees snapped off like match sticks and came flying toward us, just missing us by a couple feet. The old garage used for storage exploded, its contents swirling and flying everywhere. The entire time I was praying fervently.

In a matter of minutes it was all over. A tornado had passed through, leaving a trail of destruction. But Carl and I, and our two children were safe and sound, without a scratch on any of us. God had miraculously protected us!

Our trailer was a total loss, but we were able to salvage some items from it. The old storage garage was completely demolished. Yet, our new Ford car that had been parked in the driveway did not receive a single scratch. To our amazement, the car had apparently been lifted into the air and was set back down on top of a five gallon paint drum, which had been blown out of the garage! The can, standing upright directly underneath the axle, was actually holding the front end of the car up so that both front tires were suspended two inches above the ground!

That was a day I will never forget. I have no doubt in my mind that if God had not warned me about the coming tornado, things would have ended tragically for us that day.

Through the years, I have trusted in the Lord with all my heart and believed that everything happens for a reason. Regardless of what is taking place in my life, I know that God's arms of love are wrapped around me. I feel reassured to know we are never out of His sight!

—Sandra Wedge, Michigan

I'VE GOT SOMETHING TO TELL YOU

Years ago when my children were all still under the age of 10, my husband had an affair with a secretary in his workplace. The affair had been going on for nearly two years before I found out. They apparently had some type of falling out and split up.

When I found out about the affair, my emotional pain was almost more than I could bear and left me devastated. My husband was very sorrowful, and we jointly made the decision to stay together and attempt to work things out. Quietly, I suffered with the stinging pain of knowing my husband had been intimately involved with another woman. When around the kids and others, I tried to keep a smile on my face, but my heart was filled with despair, torment and sorrow.

One day it hit me—I had been focusing nearly all my thoughts on my husband and what had happened. I realized that my Heavenly Father and Jesus had been squeezed out of most of my thoughts. When I did talk or pray to Them, my prayers all revolved around my pain and despair.

Before I got married, my Heavenly Father and Jesus were first in my heart, life and thoughts! My days were filled with praise and worship, expressing my love and thanking Jesus and the Father for everything. Often I would memorize and quote scriptures that strengthened me. My life was filled with peace and joy then. Every day was an adventure as I lived and walked in the power, strength and joy of the Lord!

Realizing the error of my way, I set out to make my Heavenly Father and Jesus first in my life and heart again. This goal was not easy, but I knew that if I wanted to pull down the stronghold of pain that was gripping my life, I would need to bring my thoughts into obedience to Christ (2 Corinthians 10:3-5). That would mean no more dwelling on debilitating thoughts or the painful past. Instead, I would need to fix my thoughts on the Lord and what His Word says—not forgetting to spend time in prayer and praise.

In the beginning, this effort to refocus my thoughts was very difficult, but I kept it up, knowing God had promised in His Word that we could be transformed by the renewing of the thoughts in our mind (Romans 12:2). After a while, the battle became easier and my joy and peace began returning. As the months rolled on, my happiness kept increasing until finally, I knew the Lord was once again my first love.

One afternoon I was walking from the living room into the dining room, when something totally mind-boggling happened to me. God suddenly dropped a volume of information into my brain! If I were to write it all down or tell someone, it would take a while to relay the entire message—but everything God let me know was just instantly put into my head. I felt shocked and amazed!

This "revelation" concerned everything that would be happening to me that evening. The Lord revealed to me that when my husband came home from work, he would be telling me he had rented an apartment and would be moving out over the weekend. Also, my response was placed into my heart and mind.

The most astounding thing of all was that in the same instant God revealed these things to me, He also filled my heart to overflowing with supernatural joy! I felt supercharged with love, happiness, excitement, peace and the Presence of the Lord! Not one, microscopic crumb of sadness or disappointment was in my heart.

When my husband arrived home from work, I was cooking supper. Within a few minutes, he said to me, "I've got something to tell you, but I can tell you after supper."

Trying not to smile too big, I thought to myself as gleefully as a little child, *I know what it is!* Then I said to him, "Do you have to tell me later? Can you tell me now?"

Pausing a minute, he finally said, "I've rented an apartment, and I'll be moving out this weekend."

Still unable to get the smile off my face, I said, "Do you need to wait till the weekend to move out?"

He said, "No, I could move in any time now."

I said, "Well, why wait until the weekend? After supper I'll help you pack."

Once supper was over, he packed up some of his things. When he was getting ready to go out the door, I will never forget the perplexed look on his face. My response and countenance must have greatly puzzled him. My inner being was so flooded with joy that I felt like I must be glowing!

That night and the weeks that followed, my peace and joy continued—no tears, no despair or sorrow, only sweet peace. In a way, it was all very strange. For all practical purposes and to my knowledge, my husband and I had been working things out, and everything seemed to be going well.

Now, I was suddenly aware that my husband would no longer be a part of my life. I would also have the responsibility of raising the children mostly on my own. Yet neither of these realities seemed to be even of slight concern to me.

Not long after he left, I found out my husband was having another affair. With peace in my heart, I placed the situation into the Lord's hands. Soon my husband contacted me, saying he thought it best that we went on with separate lives. Feeling totally at peace, I just let him go. We probably had one of the most peaceful divorces in history!

Since that time, situations in life have sometimes caught me off guard. I catch myself focusing on things that are starting to drag me down and rob my joy, but peace is never far away. I just acknowledge that my thoughts are "out of captivity" to Christ and that my imagination has been "in captivity" to satan's lies and disheartening scenarios. Then I pray for the strength to get back on the right track and make the Lord first in my heart and mind again!

"You will keep in perfect peace all who trust in You, all whose thoughts are fixed on You!"

- Isaiah 26:3 NLT

—G. C., Michigan

TURNING POINT

At age 15, I witnessed a large goiter vanish off a woman's neck at an Oral Robert's healing service. Sitting close enough to clearly see the goiter disappear and the woman's neck instantly become flat—I almost passed out! That day was a huge turning point in my life. The reality of God's existence sank in and brought me under heavy conviction. A few days later, I knelt down on my knees and invited Jesus into my heart, and my journey of walking with the Lord began.

The years rolled on and everything seemed to be going perfectly in my life. I married my beautiful wife Kay, worked successfully in the business world, owned a nice home and car, and was involved in our church. I had everything I ever wanted. But God had other plans for me. An incident was about to happen that would change the course of my future.

Arriving home early from work one day, I had no sooner come into the house when the phone rang. My Aunt Evon was calling me from the hospital, frantically telling me that Uncle Merle was dying. Uncle Merle was my dad's brother. He used to attend church, but quit going. He had given up on God. Aunt Evon, extremely distressed, said to me, "I want you to come over here right now and pray for your uncle!" I left as quickly as I could.

After arriving at the hospital, I learned that Uncle Merle was in the Intensive Care Unit. Reluctantly, I told Aunt Evon I would not be allowed to go in and pray with him.

In a desperate plea, she nearly screamed at me, "But you've got to! Uncle Merle is dying without the Lord, and you're the only one that can get through to him!"

Again, I told Aunt Evon that the medical staff would not let me in ICU because I was not a minister. She was becoming hysterical when a doctor nearby asked me, "Can you control her?"

I told him, "All she wants me to do is go in there and pray with Uncle Merle."

The doctor said, "Go right ahead, and if anybody stops you, tell them that I sent you."

Without delay, I told Aunt Evon that I would go in and talk to Uncle Merle. Upon entering the ICU room, I was not quite prepared for what I saw. Uncle Merle looked lifeless. All color had drained from his face and arms, and he appeared to be completely unresponsive. While the attending nurse took his blood pressure, I noticed that the needle on the gauge did not move. Rather surprised, I commented, "That needle didn't move."

The nurse informed me, "If I shut the machine off right now, he's gone. He has an aneurism that broke below his heart, and it is pumping all the blood through his system and not through the arteries and veins. He's just about gone." Despite Uncle Merle's near death appearance, I told the nurse I needed to pray with him.

Over the past years, I had talked to Uncle Merle about giving his heart to the Lord. He was always going to do it "some other day." Reaching down, I took Uncle Merle's hand. It was stiff, almost colorless and cold.

In a matter-of-fact tone, I said, "Uncle Merle, I've come to pray with you. You're dying. You're almost gone, so don't give me that 'some other time.' You don't have any other time. It's over with!" Continuing on, I said, "I don't even know why I'm here, other than the fact that the Lord placed me here, and I'm here to pray with you because He still wants you!"

In that moment the reality that God still wanted Uncle Merle dawned on me and amazed me! God was not a big, mean guy with a whip, ready to snap us on the back of the head to get us to do whatever He wants us to, but a God of great love and mercy. God had always loved my uncle and placed me there to pray with him in the final minutes of his life.

I informed Uncle Merle that I was going to lead him in a prayer where he could invite Jesus to come into his heart. I reassured him, "I know you can't talk, but you can say it in your mind and it will be accepted by the Lord." With Uncle Merle's hand still in mine, I began to pray with him. Suddenly, I was astounded to feel his hand become notably warm in mine and turn a deep, pink color, in stark contrast to the rest of his body, which remained cold and ashen! Moments later, Uncle Merle was gone.

Aunt Evon and I were blessed beyond measure over this miraculous sign that Uncle Merle was able to hear me. We also believe that this was God's way of reassuring us that Uncle Merle did call out to the Lord in the final seconds of his life.

"And everyone who calls on the name of the Lord shall be saved" (Acts 2:21).

Witnessing this demonstration of God's tremendous love was another turning point in my life. From that day on, I knew I wanted to serve God with my whole heart for the rest of my days on Earth. There seemed nothing else for me to do—but become a minister!

—Charles Booth, Michigan

WITCH ON THE RUN

My good friend Lori and I were attending a fund-raiser for the family of a friend who had recently died of cancer. The large room had several rows of long, rectangular tables at which many people were seated; others were standing around. The room was filled with chatter as old acquaintances caught up with each other's lives.

Lori and I sat down on the same side of a table that was well into the room. We were busy talking when Lori spotted a young woman enter the building who was carrying an infant in a baby seat. Lori quietly mentioned to me that the woman was a witch. Lori is a devout follower of Jesus, and I knew her words were not meant as gossip. She and I have gotten together on numerous occasions to pray for our husbands, children, and others.

Surprisingly, the woman with the infant walked through the spacious room, passing up numerous empty seats to come right over to our table and sat across from us. Immediately, Lori and I struck up a friendly conversation.

As we were talking about her baby, the thought began weighing on my mind that this baby was going to be raised by a witch. Deuteronomy 18:10-11 says: "Let no one be found among you who sacrifices his son or daughter in the fire, who practices divination or sorcery, interprets omens, engages in witchcraft, or casts spells, or who is a medium or spiritist or who consults the dead." (Even so, the Lord is good, and ready to forgive; and plenteous in mercy unto all that call upon Him. Psalm 86:5 KJV)

Something began to well up inside me and I decided to pray for the baby. Not wanting the mother to suspect what I was doing, I maintained a nonchalant composure and kept a smile on my face.

Silently, I began to pray fervently. My prayer went something like, "Heavenly Father, I claim this baby's soul for Jesus. Please protect and shield her. Surround her with your angels. Please send people her way to share Your gospel with her as she grows up."

Moments after I started praying, the woman looked straight at me as if she had suddenly seen a ghost! Her eyes widened and a frightened, panicked look spread over her face. She jumped to her feet, grabbed her baby and hurried away from our table as though she were fleeing from a plague! I was startled at first. Then I began to realize what had just happened—my prayer had caused an invisible war to break out!

That incident reaffirmed to me the reality of the Bible teaching found in Ephesians 6:12 (NKJV): "For we do not wrestle against flesh and blood, but against principalities, against powers, against the rulers of the darkness of this age, against spiritual hosts of wickedness in the heavenly places." Just as we cannot see strong winds, but can observe their effect, so I could clearly observe that my prayer was riling up principalities of an unseen realm.

That day I began to look at prayer in a new light. I realized that God hears even silent prayers—and they can be powerful! Later it occurred to me, that I had probably been missing numerous opportunities to pray for others and situations throughout every day. Now, even when I hear a siren in the distance, I pray.

Since that day at the fund-raiser, I have prayed many times for that little girl and her mother. Often times, people who get involved in witchcraft, the occult, fortune-telling and related areas are seeking answers and experiences that are beyond human ability to achieve. God dearly loves all humankind, and He longs to fill the void in each of our hearts. (John 4:4-14)

After my eye-opening experience, my new motto has been, "Turn every concern and anxious thought into a prayer." When a disturbing thought pops into my mind, rather than analyze what appears to be going on, now my goal is to start praying for that situation in detail instead! Whether it is asking the Lord for divine protection, His wisdom and guidance, or whatever fits the need, praying immediately about my concerns has removed a load of anxiety, worry and fear from me. And, I have witnessed many wonderful answers to prayer!

"Do not be anxious about anything, but in everything, by prayer and petition, with thanksgiving, present your requests to God. And the peace of God, which transcends all understanding, will guard your hearts and your minds in Christ Jesus."

- Philippians 4:6-7

—Nina Stellwagen, Michigan

THE PUPPY

Before any of our children were born, my husband Mike and I got a Black Labrador puppy we named Sasha. She was an unusually loving and caring dog. When our kids came along, Sasha was wonderful with them, always gentle, never seeming to mind when they got a little carried away playing with her. Sasha was always protective of the children.

One time Sasha even took care of some kittens that we rescued from a barn, watching over them as if they were her own. Sasha was a special part of our family. When she died, we all grieved her absence.

After losing Sasha, I approached my husband Mike several times about getting another female Black Lab puppy. He always responded with, "No, not right now."

One day when my mom was babysitting the kids, our four-year-old daughter Mikehlah informed her that she was getting a puppy and that its name was going to be Angel.

My mother, knowing my husband's current stance about getting a dog, asked her, "Did your mommy and daddy tell you they were going to get you a puppy?"

With a smile on her face, she said, "No, but I asked Jesus for a puppy."

Mikehlah's comment was not a total surprise. Both my husband and I had overheard her telling various people that she had asked Jesus for a puppy. She would also inform them its name was going to be Angel. Mikehlah had been especially heartbroken when we lost Sasha and desperately wanted another dog just like her.

My desire to get a female Black Lab puppy had not diminished either. I decided to check out Craigslist.com. Narrowing my search to the Central Michigan area, I typed in "pets." To my surprise, a Labrador puppy was the first thing that came up on the list. Strangely, the location for the listing was less than ten miles from our house. Immediately, I sent an email to the owners, requesting more information and leaving them my husband's cell phone number.

Then I told Mike about my email and that I had given them his number. With a note of sarcasm, he responded, "Well, it would have to be a mighty good deal—like half price, come with toys, its own blanket, a collar, leash, kennel, not be over eight weeks old, have all its shots, be housebroken and come with a year's supply of dog food."

Thirty minutes later the woman advertising the Labrador telephoned. Mike asked her several questions and soon found out that the puppy was a black, seven-week-old female. To his amazement, he also learned that the puppy was up-to-date on all its shots, was potty trained, would come with toys, a blanket, collar, leash and kennel!

As they continued talking, the woman explained that she and her husband had purchased the dog for her mother, who—after having the puppy in her home for a week and a half—discovered she was allergic to it. Unable to keep the puppy themselves, the couple just wanted to find a good home for it as quickly as possible. The woman told Mike that everything they had purchased for the dog would be included in the package—and they were only asking half the usual price!

To Mike, this was all sounding a bit too peculiar. But the biggest surprise of all was still to come. Near the end of their phone conversation, Mike could hardly believe his ears when the woman told him her mother had named the dog "Angel." When Mike got off the phone, he said, "I think we need to go see this puppy!"

Without telling the kids what we were up to, we went to the couple's house the following morning to see the puppy. When Mike and I saw Angel, it was love at first sight! She was absolutely adorable, full of affection, licking my face all over and trying to cuddle the moment I picked her up. Soon we were filling out the paper work.

We took the puppy home and the minute Mikehlah spotted her, she began smiling from ear to ear. She said, "Is that what I think it is? Is that for me?"

Mike told her it was, then said, "Guess what her name is?"

As he opened his mouth to tell her, Mikehlah blurted out in unison with him, "Angel!"

Mike was willing to forego his stipulation about the year's supply of dog food. After all, there was not a doubt in our minds that this was God's answer to a little girl's prayers!

—Michelle Gimmey, Michigan

MARRY JERRY

In my senior year of high school, I met Jerry. He was the "new guy" at school and also a senior. All the girls thought he was really "hot," and I quickly developed a crush on him. During our Valentine's dance at school my best friend said, "If you don't ask him to dance, I will." There was no way I wanted that to happen, so I mustered up the courage to walk over to him. We danced every dance the rest of the evening.

Jerry and I fell madly in love our senior year. He asked me to marry him on graduation day. My answer was "No" and Jerry was devastated.

Marriage was completely out of the question as far as I was concerned. At a young age, I vowed to myself that I would never get married. My mother had endured a very abusive relationship with my father. When I was five years old, my dad committed suicide. During all our years growing up, my mother instilled in me and my three sisters, a strong sense of independence and that we did not need a man to live a happy, fulfilled, successful life.

At age 17, while a junior in high school, I accepted Jesus into my life. Shortly after, I informed Him that my life's desire was to be a mother. I wanted to have lots of children, just never get married. Little did I know that God had other plans for my life.

Jerry had given his life to the Lord Jesus at a Billy Graham Crusade several years before we started dating, and he was a praying man. His heartbreak over my refusal to marry him was short-lived. Unknown to me, God had spoken to Jerry's heart and told him that I would be his wife one day.

Soon after graduation, Jerry was off to the Marines in California and I moved to Mt. Pleasant, Michigan, to attend Central Michigan University (CMU). Jerry and I decided to maintain our friendship by writing letters.

For the next four years Jerry and I wrote each other weekly. During that time I let Jerry know that I had no intention of ever marrying anyone. I continually encouraged him to date and see if the Lord might have someone in California for him. He found an awesome church family, but was never interested in pursuing other women.

After serving in the Marines, Jerry moved about two hours away from Mt. Pleasant. We continued to keep in touch through phone calls and occasional visits. I was thoroughly convinced that our relationship would never become more than just friends, and I felt completely at peace about it.

Two years later Jerry decided to move to Mt. Pleasant to attend CMU and to pursue my affections. He became part of the church family that I had been a part of for the past six years. Jerry was getting a little too close for my comfort level, and I pushed him away as much as I could. Jerry was very careful to keep his motives in check with God's plans for our lives. He spent much time praying about God's timing. Much of my time was spent expressing to God how much I did not want to marry this man.

At age 27, after nine years of patiently waiting for God's timing and for me to have a serious change of heart, Jerry was ready to "go fishing." Our pastor told him there were a lot of other fish in the sea. Our pastor also came to me with some serious concerns. He told me that he believed God truly wanted to bless my life with marriage. My pastor strongly encouraged me to spend some time seriously praying about being married to Jerry.

Everything in my being did not want to marry him. Nevertheless, my desire to be obedient to God's will for my life was much stronger than my own will and plans for my life, and so I decided to go on a five-day fast. During the fast I planned to spend as much time as possible praying, reading God's Word and truly seeking His will for my future, despite my own issues.

Three days into the fast, I realized some life-changing truths. One of the reasons I never wanted to get married was a fear that marriage would detract me from my first love—Jesus. God assured me that a godly husband would only strengthen my walk with Him, and brought the scripture to my mind about a three-stranded cord: *Though one may be overpowered, two can defend themselves. A cord of three strands is not quickly broken.* (Ecclesiastes 4:12)

On the final day of my fast, something miraculous happened. Around 11:00 p.m. I was outside behind the apartment building I lived in, sitting on a small, wooden bridge that was part of a play area for kids. The playground was now abandoned due to the late hour, enabling me to spend some alone time talking to God about the whole situation with Jerry. After I had been praying for a while, I felt like I just needed to be silent and listen.

What happened next will amaze and bless me for the rest of my life! Out of the quietness, I was suddenly startled by an audible voice that said, "If you truly desire to walk in My will for your life, you will open your heart to my servant I wish to bless you with." Immediately, I looked all around me. The mercury light in the playground area clearly exposed that I was alone! The voice I heard was gentle, loving, soothing, yet authoritative.

All my fears and doubts melted away at that moment. My mind and heart were suddenly filled with the knowledge that I was going to marry Jerry. My mind held not a shadow of a doubt that it was God's perfect plan for me. Happiness, joy and peace seemed to sweep over me—an unforgettable, life-changing moment.

Excitedly, I ran into the building to my apartment that I shared with three other girls. I couldn't wait to tell them what had just happened. We all rejoiced together about the remarkable thing the Lord had just done!

Jerry and I began dating and diligently praying about the Lord's direction for our life together. We were engaged one month later on February 14, nine years to the day of our first dance together in high school! During our courtship and engagement, the Lord helped me to fall so much in love with this amazing, awesome, godly man. Three months later, we were married.

After more than twenty years of marriage, I am still thankful for my husband every day. I continue to feel humbled that God would give me such a wonderful, godly man to love me so much. Jerry enhances and strengthens my life and walk with the Lord more than I could ever imagine. That Jerry was patient and faithful enough to wait nine years for me, leaves me speechless and forever grateful to this day. God also fulfilled my heart's desire to be a mother and blessed Jerry and me with three wonderful kids. God is so amazing!

—Pam, Michigan

THE BIRTHDAY PRESENT

It was Sunday morning, and it was my birthday. As usual on Sundays, I planned to go to church. After getting ready, I walked outside to get in my car and was shocked to discover that it had three flat tires! I felt very upset. Being a single female didn't help matters any.

After calling the police and filing a report, I learned that vandals had slashed the tires on about 25 cars during the night. That my car had to be one of them was disheartening to me. Filling out the paper work and not having a car to drive, seemed such an inconvenience.

My car was towed to an auto service center to have the damaged tires replaced. Upon examining the fourth tire that had appeared at first to be OK, it was discovered that it, too, had been slashed, and so it was replaced as well. My insurance covered everything except a $50 deductible, which a member of my church graciously insisted on paying for me.

After all was said and done, I was pondering over my long difficult day, when it suddenly dawned on me that I had recently asked God for new tires. The existing ones were getting worn and needed to be replaced before winter. As a single person living on a modest income, buying four new tires would have been impossible for me. I finally realized that not only had God given me the four new tires I asked for—He gave them to me on my birthday!

—Lisa B., Michigan

CATHERINE'S COMFORT

NOTE FROM THE EDITOR: Several years ago, I purchased the movie "A Man Called Peter," based on the life of Peter Marshall, a Scottish-born American preacher. The movie has become one of my all-time favorites, depicting the love that Peter and his wife Catherine had for God and for one another and the obstacles they faced and overcame in ministry and in life. The movie was produced in Hollywood in 1955 and is still available in many Christian bookstores.

A few years ago, I had the opportunity to read A Man Called Peter, written by Catherine Marshall (Peter's wife), which was the inspiration for the movie. While reading chapter 20, I felt very touched as Catherine described the supernatural comfort God gave her following Peter's unexpected death.

With the gracious permission of Peter and Catherine's son, Peter John Marshall, Catherine's account of her experience has been included in this book.

To set the stage: Peter and Catherine were married in 1936. Soon Peter became the pastor of the New York Avenue Presbyterian Church in Washington, DC. In 1947, in addition to his clerical position, Peter began serving as the United States' Senate Chaplain.

On January 26, 1949, Peter awoke in the middle of the night with severe pain in his chest and arms. He called out to Catherine, asking that she call the doctor. An ambulance arrived shortly to take Peter to the hospital. At Peter's request, Catherine did not go along to the hospital but remained at home with their young son Peter. Early the following morning Catherine received a call from the doctor—Peter had slipped into eternity.

Catherine should have been filled with grief and sorrow, but she reports that God encompassed her with an extraordinary sense of His love and presence that began right after the ambulance left with Peter. The following is Catherine's account of her divine visitation, excerpted from Chapter 20 of A Man Called Peter.

After the ambulance had gone, I went back upstairs and knelt by my bed. But before I could speak a word, there surged through me, over and around me, as a great wave, an overwhelming experience of the love of God. It was as if the Everlasting Arms were literally enfolding me. It seemed unnecessary to ask God for anything. I simply gave Peter and myself into the care and keeping of that great love. At the time, I thought this meant that Peter's heart would be healed here on earth. Of course, God knew what I did not know. There, in the lower hall, just before the ambulance left, I had seen Peter alive for the last time.

It was eight-fifteen that morning that Peter stepped over into the Larger Life. At eight-twenty the doctor telephoned to tell me. Little Peter had been making final preparations for school. He was by the phone as I got the news, and burst into a flood of little-boy tears. I was much too stunned to weep.

Later, I sat for an hour by Peter's hospital bed. He had been dozing and had slipped away very peacefully.

I felt I knew what happened before I got there. All at once, Peter had seen the Lord, and later, his own father, whom he had longed all of his life to know. There had been moments of quiet adoration and of glad reunion. Then suddenly, Peter had realized. He was dead!

"You know, this will be hard for Catherine," he had said. "What can we do for her?" And Jesus smiled at Peter. "She'll be all right. We can supply her with every resource she needs."

So, they waited for me there. That was why, when I opened the door and stepped quietly into the bare little hospital room, it was filled with the glory of God and with two vivid, transcendent Presences. Peter was not in the still form, but was hovering near in tenderness and in love.

I sat for a long time by the bed holding his hand. After a while there came a gentle tap on the door. It was A. D. [a close friend of Catherine's]. I beckoned her to come in. Her eyes seemed glued to my face. Days later, I learned why—what she had seen there. She stayed just a minute, then left.

There came a specific time, exactly fifty minutes by my wrist watch after I entered the hospital room, when those two luminous Presences left me. Suddenly, the room was empty, cheerless, cold, and I shivered. It was time for me to leave, too.

As I rose to go, I knew this was farewell to the earthly part of this man I loved; farewell to the touch of his hand, to his warmth, his gaiety, his flashing smile.

Catherine reports that for the next few days after Peter's death, God carried her in His supernatural strength.

But for a few days at least it was not dark in the Valley of the Shadow. My path was lit by celestial light. Around me was all the glory of heaven. It was as if Peter, joyously stepping over that invisible boundary that divides this life from the next, had left the curtain pulled aside, letting heaven through so that we, who were left here, could share a little of his joy and understand better what was happening to him.

For the first time, I was actually living in the kingdom of God on earth. Many decisions had to be made. There was perfect guidance for all of them. No groping to know God's will on this or that was necessary. There was just a sure, immediate, inner knowing of the right thing to do.

Though I did not sleep at all that first night, in the morning every detail of the funeral service was clear to me, even to the Scripture to be used.

Later, Catherine received a letter from A. D., her close friend who had briefly come into the hospital room after Peter's death. The following is an excerpt from that letter.

Catherine, my dear, my dear ...

I don't think you have any idea how transformed you were in that hour. I have never seen you look so beautiful. The smile that was on your face was my first glimpse of the heavenly glory which surrounded every part of Peter's going. I know you well enough to know when something has been added to you, and you were unquestionably filled with a newness and a difference, and all the love in the world was in your eyes.

That room was filled with the same power that was in you. It was charged with it. I shall never be able to thank you enough for asking me to come in. It was in those moments that I learned what Christ's power over death is. Glory filled that room.

Jesus said . . . *"I am the resurrection and the life. He who believes in Me, though he may die, he shall live. And whoever lives and believes in Me shall never die. Do you believe this?"*
- *John 11:25-26, NKJV*

In loving memory of Peter and Catherine
Peter, 1902-1949
Catherine, 1914-1983

Peter John Marshall
1940-2010

Reverend Peter John Marshall passed away unexpectedly September 8, 2010. He had devoted himself to a nationwide ministry of preaching, teaching and writing, with the desire of helping restore America to its Bible-based foundations. He co-authored three best-selling books: *The Light and The Glory, From Sea to Shining Sea, and Sounding Forth the Trumpet.*

—Nina Stellwagen, Michigan

LOST BOOK

NOTE FROM THE EDITOR: The previous story, Catherine's Comfort, was not written without a challenge and WOW story of its own.

The original 1951 copy of *A Man Called Peter* was one I had borrowed from my parents. Since it was published nearly six decades ago, it occurred to me that many people had never read the book.

Catherine's description of the supernatural comfort God gave her surrounding Peter's death greatly encouraged me. We all are aware of the deep pain and sorrow one would normally experience when suddenly and unexpectedly losing a dear loved one. Yet, directly after Peter's death, God let Catherine experience a wave of His love and joy which she described as: "Around me was all the glory of heaven … " Such a divine encounter reminds us that God's joy-filled kingdom exists and is only a breath away for His children.

To include Catherine's story in the Wow Stories book became a desire of my heart—but not a simple task. I would have to get permission from Peter and Catherine's son, Peter John, who was a young boy when his father died in 1949. How could I find him? If I were able to locate him, would he give his consent to print the story?

As these thoughts were going through my mind, I stepped into our home office to get something. A radio had been left on. I was about to walk out of the room, when the announcer's unexpected words rang like music in my ears: "Today's guest is Peter Marshall, son of the late Peter Marshall, former Senate Chaplain." Overjoyed, I grabbed an ink pen and listened intently for any contact information. At the end of the interview when a website was given, I concluded God was opening a door.

Knowing it would be wise to have a completed story with correct quotes from Catherine's book for Mr. Marshall's inspection; I went without delay to get my copy of *A Man Called Peter* from the small hutch in our living room. Although I was sure I had stored it in the hutch, the book was not there. We have two bookcases upstairs in our home, which I immediately went and searched without success.

For unfortunate reasons, the book would have been easy to spot. Rudy, the small German Pinscher we adopted from an animal shelter, had chewed on the hardcover copy of Catherine's book—among other books—when left alone for the first time. The first part of the title "A Man" had been eaten away from the dark, hunter green spine, exposing a light cream color underneath. Only the words "Called Peter" were visible. A small portion of the bottom of the spine had also been chewed off. Needless to say, the book should have stuck out like a sore thumb!

After Rudy's book demolition incident, I had put the damaged book in the hutch. From time to time, I would take it out and reread Catherine's touching account in chapter 20 concerning Peter's death. Now, when I desperately needed her book, I could not find it.

Anxious to get started writing the story, I conducted several in-depth searches for the book—each time becoming more baffled and frustrated. At least twice, I took all the books out of the hutch, and then put them back, one by one. On a few occasions, I got down on my hands and knees to scan the titles in each shelf of our bookcases. It seemed as though *A Man Called Peter* had vanished from our home. The idea of tracking down the book on the Internet, then waiting for it to arrive in the mail—knowing I already had a copy somewhere in the house—irritated me.

One day, after completing another detailed search to no avail, I came downstairs, plopped into a chair in the living room and cried out in sheer frustration, "OK, Lord, the book is lost. I don't know where it could possibly be, but You know right where it is. Would You please just stick it in one of the bookcases for me?" Then, I marched back upstairs to the nearest bookcase and, instantly, the first book my eyes were drawn to was, of course, *A Man Called Peter*. The rest is history. God never ceases to amaze me!

—Nina Stellwagen, Michigan

HIP HIP HURRAY

In 1955, after giving birth to six boys, my mother finally gave birth to me, a bouncing baby girl! The seven of us were born within nine years. My parents had four more children after me, two girls and two boys, for a total of eleven children.

Immediately after I was born, my mother and the delivery doctor noticed that my one leg hung down lower than the other leg. Soon a condition described as "malposition of the head of the femur in the acetabulum" was diagnosed—a position that prevents the hip joint from forming properly. If not taken care of early, the condition can lead to a walking disability later in life.

Amazingly, the femur bone in infants can be manipulated close to the pelvic bone and a new hip will form. This surgery, called "closed reduction of the hip," was performed on me within six weeks after my birth. I was put in a body cast from the hips down to the ankle. An opening in the cast allowed for care of bodily functions. A cast was necessary for three years and was replaced during that time as often as required to keep up with my growth.

Although the surgery was successful, it resulted in my one leg being slightly longer than the other. This did not affect my physical abilities or range of motion in any way as I was growing up. In my teen years, I became a cheerleader.

But in my late 40s, I noticed my one knee hurting a bit when I jogged. The condition worsened until it became difficult to jog and excruciatingly painful to kneel down. Consequently, I became less active and exercised much less. From time to time, I would pray about the pain, with little or no results.

Late one night in 2005, something extraordinary happened. At 11:00 p.m. I began watching the 700 Club on TV. Shortly after the program started, I fell into a deep sleep. Suddenly, a few minutes before midnight, I woke up just in time to hear Gordon Robertson and Terry Meeuwsen, the hosts of the program, praying for people with physical ailments. Gordon said he felt God wanted to heal someone with a knee problem. I was not quite sure the healing was for me until Terry said, "It's not just a knee problem, it's from the past and it involves their knee, leg and hip."

As soon as I realized the healing was for me, faith rose up in me. Instantly what felt like a jolt of electricity went through the top of my head, down my whole right side, into my hip, leg, knee and, finally, my foot. I knew I was healed!

After Gordon finished praying, he said, "If you have received your healing, do something you couldn't do before." Immediately, I fell on my knees and, sure enough, there was no pain whatsoever! My husband was sound asleep in our bedroom when I woke him up to tell him I had been healed. Excitedly, I ran around the house crying and praising God, exclaiming, "I'm healed! I'm healed!"

Since my healing, I have never again felt even a trace of pain in my knee! I have resumed jogging, bike riding and other physical activities I had once enjoyed. On my 53rd birthday, I even went skydiving!

Being able to do these things has been wonderful, but just as exciting is what this experience has taught me about God. At the time in my life when my healing occurred, I was not seeking a miracle for my knee. I had only been trying to get close to God by praying, reading my Bible and striving to do whatever might draw me closer to Him. My surprise healing made me realize that God was aware of my pain and that He cared about every detail of my life. Never before had I felt so loved!

Another thing I learned was that God's healing power is not limited by time or space. I had been watching a rerun of the 700 Club when Gordon and Terry's words were spoken!

God may not do everything when and how we think He should, but I have come to realize that He knows all things and has perfect timing for everything. Praise God!

"And we know that in all things God works for the good of those who love him, who have been called according to his purpose."

- Romans 8:28

"He has made everything beautiful in its time."

- Ecclesiastes 3:11a

—Mary Ann Miiller, Michigan

SEVENFOLD

My husband Bob and I were long-time members of the Christian and Missionary Alliance Church, known for its involvement with world missions. Once our four children were grown, we accepted our own call to the mission field and were given the opportunity to serve God in a way that seemed perfectly suited for both of us.

My husband and I would be running a missionary guesthouse in Cali, Colombia—a place where missionaries could rest and recover from their hard labor. The guesthouse also provided traveling missionaries a safe and restful place to stay. My husband Bob was excellent at bookkeeping and administrative tasks, while I loved to cook and clean, and was gifted in domestic organizational skills. We were to be missionaries to the missionaries. Hopefully, we would lighten their burdens, enabling them to be refreshed before returning to their own mission stations.

One of the requirements for entering the mission field was that we be debt free. After selling most of our possessions and paying all our existing bills, we had little money left. The mission board advised us to load our "missionary barrels" with practical items beneficial for the guest house in Cali that might not be available or were too expensive in Colombia. The $100.00 left in my checking account did not seem like enough to purchase these things.

With only a couple weeks left to get everything in order, God impressed on my heart to give the remaining money in my account to a radio ministry called *Haven of Rest*, that had blessed me throughout the years. It seemed untimely of God to want me to give the last $100.00 in my bank account to another ministry when so many useful things needed to be purchased for Colombia.

No matter how much I rationalized about how productively the money could be used for our own coming venture, I could not escape the feeling that God wanted me to give it to the other ministry. Deciding to obey God's voice, I wrote the check out for $100.00, leaving the balance at zero. Since our mailman was due to come soon, I put the check and a short note into an envelope and addressed it.

When I saw the mailman approaching our house, I stepped outside to hand him my letter. In exchange, he handed me our mail, including one from the Metropolitan District Ladies of New York. Upon opening it up, to my great surprise I found a check made out to my husband and me for $700.00! A letter inside explained that they were a group of Christian and Missionary Alliance women who try to supply some of the needs of missionaries. The enclosed donation was to help with some of the upcoming expenses they knew we would incur.

God is such a wonderful provider! Through the years I have learned one lesson over and over again—you can't out-give God!

—Dolly Straley, Florida

GET UP, NOELLE

At 19 years old, I married a crop farmer. Early that same year we overhauled the farm by cleaning, painting, and clearing out buildings, barns and corncribs, in preparation for bringing in livestock and expanding the farm.

One stormy evening we finished clearing a large, old barn. I had just completed sweeping down cobwebs from the thick cement walls and rafters when I sat down on a cooler to rest. The cooler sat about four feet away from the wall. Looking around, I was admiring the now empty, clean barn.

Suddenly, I felt a soft tap on my back and heard a voice close to my ear quietly say, "Get up, Noelle." Yet there was no one behind me! The voice, gentle and caring, felt as though it came from someone I had known all of my life—someone I could trust 100 percent. Without hesitation, I instantly stood to my feet and slid my cooler over about five feet.

The very moment I plopped back down on the cooler, a thunderous, violent BOOM sounded, as if a bomb had exploded. An old window—encased in heavy iron—had been caught by the wind and blown out of the barn wall. It crashed onto the floor, landing precisely where I had been sitting moments before!

Speechless, I sat there staring at the shattered glass and old iron window frame. Thankful and amazed, I knew God had protected me.

From time to time, I think about that day and how God spared me. The fact that God saved me from death or serious injury comforts me. The incident has left me with the sense that God kept me alive for a reason and that He must still have some things for me to do.

—Noelle Shaw, Michigan

ARMY BLANKETS

I was lying in bed around 11:30 pm, sleepy, but still talking to God, when the phone rang. My friend Ron called to inform me that we needed to make a rescue.

Both of us are part of a men's group under Faith Walkers Ministries. We are a group of men who have given our hearts to the Lord and have made a pact to look out for each other and to hold one another accountable. Our goal is to live victorious lives for Jesus Christ.

We often call each other for moral support and have agreed that if any of us falls into a temptation that could harm us spiritually, others in our group will come to the rescue and do what we can to help the struggling brother. Often that means attempting to get him out of an undesirable situation, then staying, praying, and talking with him until the crisis has passed. Most of our rescues have been in bars and crack houses.

The minute Ron told me where our rescue was to take place, I knew it was not going to go over too well with my wife Tammy. This rescue would happen at a strip club. I have done a lot of rescues, but never in a strip bar. Ron had received the phone call concerning a "brother" whose car was seen parked at Foxy Lady.

Quietly, I told my wife that Ron and I needed to make a rescue. When Tammy asked me where the rescue would be, I mumbled, "At the Foxy Lady," secretly hoping she would not hear me.

Unable to understand what I said, she asked me again, "Where?"

In a barely audible voice, I told her again, "The Foxy Lady." This went on for a minute until Tammy finally understood me and then, as I suspected, she responded with a burst of emotion: "You're not going to the Foxy Lady! This can't be God! He wouldn't want you to go in there!" Tammy continued her argument until she was interrupted by a phone call. It was Ron's wife Lea, wanting to talk with her.

Lea said to Tammy, "If our husbands are making a rescue at the Foxy Lady, we need to cover them with prayer." Immediately the peace of God came over Tammy, and she said to me, "Go—before I change my mind." The girls remained on the phone praying as I went out the door.

Ron was waiting for me in the driveway. He was fairly new at making rescues. After a quick briefing, I told him the most important thing that we needed to do was get prayed up before we left.

We sat in Ron's car for 15 to 20 minutes, praying fervently. I was praying so diligently that my feet were bouncing on the floor. Part of our prayers included asking God to protect us, to blind us from being able to see any nudity and to keep us from getting tempted. We prayed about every detail the Holy Spirit brought to our minds until we knew in our hearts that it was time to go. On the way, we continued to pray, sing and praise God.

When we arrived at Foxy Lady, we parked the car and then walked into the main entrance. Neither one of us had ever been in there before. Silently, we continued to pray with every step we took.

A bouncer stood just inside the door. Our eyes met and I simply said to him, "We're here to rescue a brother." He nodded, giving us the go ahead to continue. Next, we came to a girl who was collecting the entrance fee. Again, I said nothing more than, "We're here to rescue a brother." She let us pass without paying.

In the center of the room were several tables with men sitting at them. Along the far wall were more tables where we spotted our brother. We walked directly over to where he was and sat down by him, Ron on one side and me on the other. He looked shocked to see us and asked, "What are you doing in here?!"

Bluntly, I told him, "I'm here to get you."

He said, "I can't leave. I'm here with my friends."

Filled with a boldness and confidence from God, I said, "You've got three minutes. The clock's ticking. You need to make a decision!" The Lord continued to put words into my mouth. I said, "You've stumbled. The Lord loves you. He will forgive you, but you need to get out of here!" Glancing at my watch, I told him, "You've got a minute and a half left. You need to choose!"

At that point, I let him know we were leaving and would be waiting outside, and that his time was running out. As Ron and I headed for the door, I noticed an unusual sight—three or four girls wrapped up in army blankets. At the time, it seemed odd, but I never gave it a second thought.

Outside the club, I looked at my watch again—less than half a minute left for our brother to heed his warning. I was still staring at my watch, observing the final countdown until one second to go, when the club door opened and out came our brother! Teary-eyed, he said, "I'm ready. Let's go." Ron and I were praising God and rejoicing!

We took our brother to a coffee shop to sober him up. We spent a few hours talking and praying with him. At some point in our conversation, I mentioned how strange it was to see girls in the club, wrapped in army blankets. Ron agreed, also thinking it peculiar. Our rescued brother looked at us as if we were crazy. That is when Ron and I realized that none of the girls were wrapped in army blankets. Only Ron and I saw the blankets!

Later, I found out that while Tammy and Lea were praying over the phone, they specifically asked the Lord to cover up the girls. God is so awesome!

Afterward, while marveling over what God had done and wondering why He had chosen army blankets to cover the girls, God spoke to my heart to let me know: He was our commanding officer and Ron and I were His soldiers. We were at war, sent on a mission, and He had our back. How fitting for God to use army blankets to cover the girls, as well as to be protective coverings for Ron and me. It is hard to put into words how much this miracle has blessed my wife and me.

"Because he loves me," says the LORD, "I will rescue him; I will protect him, for he acknowledges my name. He will call upon me, and I will answer him; I will be with him in trouble, I will deliver him and honor him."

- Psalm 91:14-15

—Rossi Borgia, Florida

AMAZING LOVE

At the age of 16, I gave my heart to Jesus at a youth camp. I felt like a new person and was fired up to follow Jesus. But it was not long before I was back to my old ways.

By the time I was in my early 20s, my life had reached an all-time low. The party scene had lost its allure, and I learned that often people could not be trusted. I also ended a three-year relationship with my boyfriend. Soon after this breakup, I moved into a cheap apartment in a very undesirable part of town. Almost every night I could hear people arguing and fighting. There were occasions when I feared for my life.

My single-person income left me so financially strapped that I could not afford a phone or TV. I didn't have so much as a spare dime to spend at a garage sale. To top things off, I totaled my car and had no transportation, which meant walking to work every day, rain or shine. Anxiety, worry, fear and anger constantly plagued my mind.

Deep in my heart, I knew God was the only answer to the miserable rut I had fallen into.

The only piece of literature in my apartment was a Bible my parents had given me. I decided to read it and do whatever it said, hoping it would somehow fix my messed-up life.

As I began reading in the New Testament, I quickly discovered there were numerous things I had been doing wrong. With determination, I set out to be a "good" person.

One day I read a verse in the Bible that said, "Whatever is true, whatever is noble, whatever is right, whatever is pure, whatever is lovely, whatever is admirable, if anything is excellent or praiseworthy, think about such things." (Philippians 4:8)

When I attempted to think my first praiseworthy thought, to my total dismay absolutely nothing came to mind! Everything I had been thinking involved my financial woes, fears of being raped or murdered where I lived, anger and resentment towards my ex-boyfriend, loneliness, etc. Many of the things I had been thinking were true, but they were in no way noble, pure, lovely, admirable, excellent or praiseworthy.

The greatest mental battle I have ever faced began when I attempted to think only good thoughts! This meant I was no longer supposed to dwell on the things that worried, scared, angered or upset me. I had to wrack my brain to come up with a single praiseworthy thought!

As the months rolled on, I felt better. I often prayed for people, read my Bible daily and even cultivated new attitudes toward others—but something was still missing in my life.

At some point it dawned on me: if Jesus is real, I should be able to talk with Him as I would with any close friend. My prayers had mostly been long, ritualized lists of requests. Instead, I began talking to Jesus, expressing everything in my heart as though He were right beside me. Soon I began telling Jesus regularly that I loved Him, and I thanked Him for everything I could think of.

At first, I felt no change. But sensing that I was being tested in some way, I kept it up.

After a while, the sweetest peace began to infiltrate my heart and mind, and I began to experience a new joy I had never known before. It was exhilarating! Sometimes I felt like I could jump up and touch a 20-foot ceiling! Jesus had become my closest, dearest friend. Never before had I known such a great and personal love!

One day, while still living in my apartment, I noticed what appeared to be a small, red boil on my face. Months passed by and it never went away. I decided to go to a dermatologist and get it checked out. A biopsy revealed that what looked like a boil was only the tip of an underlying mass of cancer.

A surgery date was scheduled. Diagrams were drawn to prepare me emotionally for the significant amount of tissue that was going to be removed from my face.

The night before my surgery, while sitting on my bed talking to Jesus and telling Him I loved Him, I nonchalantly said, "Jesus, if You wanted to heal me, You could." Immediately the words "I do," were directly communicated to my mind. At that moment I felt encompassed by an electrifying Presence as waves of love and joy pulsated through me and all around me! Then I felt a hand reach into my face and pull the cancer out! Filled with indescribable happiness, I knew beyond any doubt the cancer was gone—Jesus had removed it!

The following morning when I went to my scheduled surgery, I had total confidence that the cancer was no longer there. As the surgical staff began to administer the anesthesia, I said to them, "You won't find it cuz Jesus took it out." When I regained consciousness, I was informed that they could find NO cancer.

As remarkable as this miracle was, what touched my heart the most was that God demonstrated His power and love to me on the heels of the most sinful, disobedient time of my life. Truly, He had forgiven all my sins "and remembered them no more" (Psalm 103:10-13). Who can fathom God's amazing love?

"You are forgiving and good, O Lord, abounding in love to all who call to You."

- Psalm 86:5

—Nina Stellwagen, Michigan

LIVER TRANSPLANT

Born and raised in Florida, my early childhood was a bittersweet experience. My father died of a heart attack when I was a year old. My mother worked as a waitress to support my sisters and me. Although we were dirt poor, Mom did her best to make a wonderful home life for us. She also took us kids to Sunday school and church every week.

When I was nine years old, my mother remarried. Since I longed for a father figure in my life, I was happy about the marriage. A year later, my stepfather died.

Around the age of 14, I tried alcohol for the first time. By age 15, drinking was a regular part of my life. One day while waiting at the school bus stop, some of the kids were smoking dope, and I decided to try some. I was instantly hooked.

After that, I began skipping school and smoking pot in addition to my drinking. Around this time, I became angry with God, blaming Him for the deaths of my father and step-dad, for our poverty, and for everything that was not going well in my life. With growing resentment against God, I began drinking as often as possible.

At age 17, I got my girlfriend pregnant. Our family philosophy was, if you got a girl in trouble, you needed to marry her. With both of us still in our teens, we were married. But my drinking continued, and I knew nothing about being a good husband.

Although I had a job working in construction and was making good money, the vast majority of my paycheck was squandered on alcohol and drugs. Much of my spare time was spent in bars drinking with my coworkers. Frequently, I worked all day, went straight to the bars and drank all night, then went back to work in the morning without going home. Hanging out with the guys seemed to fulfill that male bonding thing that I longed for.

When my son was born, it felt like the greatest moment of my life. After watching his birth in the delivery room, I cried like a baby.

But, a week later, I was drinking up the formula and diaper money. We would have to borrow money from family to get the baby's necessities. I wanted to be a good father, but alcohol had taken full-blown control over me. Our marriage was not going well, and we were often fighting.

Around the age of 19, I started doing cocaine. Soon I began selling cocaine to support my own habit, while continuing to drink every day. The money I made at my job, that should have been used to pay rent and household bills, was spent on drugs and alcohol.

As a result, my wife, son and I moved from place to place. Finally, we moved into a barn behind my mother's house that I fixed into a makeshift apartment. Because there was no indoor plumbing, we had to use the bathrooms and water in my mom's house. Five years into our marriage, my wife filed for divorce. After she divorced me, any control I thought I had over my drinking was gone.

My life continued to go downhill. After a while, I started hanging around with people who were into witchcraft and Satanism. I involved myself in deviant practices and denied God's existence. My thinking became so twisted that I remember wanting to give people the impression that I was insane and dangerous.

By the time I was in my mid-30s, my life had racked up a long list of jail times—bar fight injuries, including being stabbed numerous times—enough DUIs to be facing a potential five-year prison sentence—many short-term relationships that included my arrest for domestic violence—several jobs lost because I stole from my employers—and homelessness.

I was a poor excuse for a human being and had reached the bottom of the bottom, destroying many lives in the process. Because of the person I'd become, I isolated myself from my family, calling my mom on the phone maybe once a year, and that was likely to get bail money.

Despite my drinking and drug addictions, I always worked and did my best at my job. One week my boss in South Carolina sent the entire crew home for a week's vacation. At age 36, I had no home of my own, so I planned to stay with my sister in Cape Coral, Florida.

My first day back in my home state, I met up with old friends and got drunk. Afterward I went to my sister's and slept on her couch. The following morning I had a stomachache. By the time my sister returned home from work that evening, I was curled up in a ball on the floor with excruciating pain and a fever of 105°.

My sister took me to the hospital. Everyone assumed my appendix had ruptured. After many tests, the doctor came into my room, very upset and stern. She told me that I was in the end stage of cirrhosis of the liver, and that even if I never drank another drop of alcohol, I might live six months. If I drank again, I would be dead in less than six months. The doctor also told me I had Hepatitis C.

For the first time in my life, I truly wanted to quit drinking. Never before had anything inspired me enough to lay it down. Alcohol had been my solution to every problem. If I was lonely or angry, alcohol comforted me. If I was happy, it made things better. Alcohol had been my best friend for my entire adult life. Now, I was given six months to live, and I was scared!

I remained in the hospital for the next 15 days with the doctor's prognosis weighing heavily in my thoughts. With every fiber of my being, I was determined to never drink again. Yet, the day I was released from the hospital, I wound up getting drunk, intending only to say goodbye to my friends at the bar.

After waking up the next day, I had to face the truth: I was powerless to stop drinking and had no control over my own life. In the past, I was checked into various drug rehab facilities and went to some programs, because of court orders, not because I wanted to. Now I wanted help. I decided to go to a 12-step program. At this time in my life, God began divinely intervening and did a series of mini miracles on my behalf.

From past experience, I knew the 12-step program would involve seeking a Higher Power. Since I still held resentment toward God, I did not want anyone talking to me about Him! So, when it came to choosing someone to be my sponsor, I looked around the room and saw a guy that looked like the meanest, toughest man there. John was bald with a goatee and covered with tattoos. Confidently, I thought to myself, "This guy won't talk about God. I'll ask him to be my sponsor."

If I would have looked a little closer at some of his tattoos, I might have noticed that many of them were crosses and things to do with Jesus. God was practically all John talked about! John was a former hardcore alcoholic. I could see he had recovered and appeared to be happy. He understood where I was and knew what I needed to hear. God had hand-picked the perfect person to be my sponsor!

John and I met on a weekly basis. One of the things he asked me to do was to get on my knees every morning and ask God to help me stay sober for just one day. And if I stayed sober that day, I was to get on my knees that night and thank God for keeping me sober that day. Because I was desperate, I did what John asked. Every week he would ask me how I was doing and if I was still praying.

One day John asked me, "Do you have any faith that God is going to remove this from you?"

I told him bluntly, "No, I don't. I believe it works for you people, but it doesn't work for me."

Then he asked me, "How long have you been sober since you started praying every day?" After thinking about it, I realized I had been sober for three months!

I answered, "Three months."

Then John asked me the trick question, "How long could you stay sober before you started praying?" He already knew the answer because I had told him my story. For the past 20 years, I could not stay sober for a single day unless I was locked up in a treatment facility, behind bars, or in a hospital bed.

Suddenly, I had an overwhelming awareness that God was working in my life. I couldn't understand why, but I could not argue with the evidence! This caused my prayers to change. I continued to ask God to keep me sober every morning and thanked Him each night. But I began to add in other things. I asked God to guide my thoughts, for direction in my life, and to help me treat others the way I would have them treat me. And I began asking God to show me where, in my daily life, I could be of service to Him.

Although many of the things John had been saying were getting through to me, I still felt like one of the worst people on the planet. I believed I was unforgivable and that, in reality, God would not want me.

Then one day when my sister was driving me somewhere, I saw a sign in front of a church that had the Bible scripture John 3:16 written on it: "For God so loved the world that he gave his one and only Son, that whoever believes in him shall not perish but have eternal life."

The meaning hit me like a tidal wave, and I started bawling like a baby. Alarmed, my sister pulled the car over and started asking: "What's wrong?! What's wrong?!"

Barely able to talk, I said, "God loves me!" Numerous times during my life, I had heard John 3:16, but it had never become real to me until that moment. The reality of God's love—that there was nothing I could do that was beyond His forgiveness, nothing that could keep me from His love, that Jesus was there for me, waiting, and all I had to do was ask Him into my life—finally sank in! From that day on, I started the marvelous journey of making Jesus my Lord and Savior.

Shortly after that day, I started going to church. I still had fears about dying and about my probable prison sentence for my fourth DUI. But on the day I was baptized, when I came up out of the water, all the fears from my entire life left me! My health remained in serious jeopardy, but I had a new peace in my heart. Many people in my church now prayed for me.

At six months sobriety, I had my DUI hearing. I told the judge about my health situation and threw myself at the mercy of the court. Out of a possible five-year prison sentence, the court gave me the shortest sentence they could possibly give me of 30 days in jail!

Because of my poor health, I had been told to not work or even lift more than five pounds, but I couldn't stand not working. Six months after I was supposed to be dead, I went back to work for a past employer, who graciously rehired me, even though I had stolen from him. An income made it possible to work at making amends for my past dishonest dealings.

My job had insurance coverage, which would not cover any preexisting conditions until I had been on it one full year. On the 365th day, after working at that job for exactly one year, when my insurance coverage kicked in, I started bleeding and vomiting blood at work.

Rushed to the hospital, I was given 18 units of blood, and had an emergency operation. An artery in my esophagus had ruptured and was pumping blood into my stomach. Three days later the hospital discharged me. I went home and started vomiting blood again. When the ambulance arrived, my body temperature was 82—and my blood pressure was 30/15. That day I received 22 more units of blood and had another emergency operation. My life was spared again. This time I spent a month in the hospital.

A liver transplant was essential to my survival. I now had the necessary insurance, but with my past drinking history and arrests, my chances of being put on the list for a liver transplant were slim to nothing. I asked a couple people to write me a letter of recommendation. To my great surprise, 200 people wrote letters! Not only that, a petition was circulated requesting I be given a liver transplant, which 200 people signed. I didn't think I knew that many people. My name was put on the list for a liver transplant!

My hospitalizations became numerous and frequent. The church continued to pray for me and frequently came to visit me whenever I was in the hospital. None of my old friends ever came. My condition had deteriorated to the point that I was missing weeks out of my life, unaware time had passed. Before my liver failure, I was physically strong, working hard for years in construction and weighing 265 pounds. Now I was lying helplessly in a hospital bed, weighing 109 pounds and unable to walk.

Then I was transferred to Cedars Hospital in Miami. While there, I felt more alert—possibly because Cedars specialized in caring for terminally ill patients. I remember spending many long, comforting nights talking to God and reading my Bible during the months I waited for a liver.

On July 2, 2002, two years after I stopped drinking and a year and a half past my survival expectancy, a liver came in that was a perfect match for me. Two men were ahead of me on the list to receive a transplant. When the first candidate reacted badly to the anesthesia, doctors knew he would not survive the transplant. For reasons unknown to me, in a last minute decision, I was put in the number one spot.

Everything began happening fast. I was transferred across the street to the University of Miami Hospital, where the transplant would take place. With so much action going on—22 people in the room, many of them working on me—I did not have time to think. When the staff had finished prepping me for the operation, my bed was wheeled into a room. Suddenly I was all alone. Fear began to creep in. Anxious thoughts plagued my mind: "Am I going to survive this? What if I don't make it through the surgery?"

My family had been notified, but would not be able to arrive before the surgery started. I began to feel very alone, as though I had forgotten everything I learned about how the Lord would always be with me.

The anesthesiologist came in and started talking to me. I told him how God had changed my life, and that I was a recovering alcoholic.

The anesthesiologist began saying the most comforting things to me—as though his words were a gift from God. When it was time for him to administer the anesthesia, he took hold of my hand and said, "How about if I say a prayer?" To this day, I believe God sent that man to me, to say the exact words I needed to hear during the loneliest, most frightening time of my life.

Two days later, I woke up. The liver transplant was a total success and my rapid recovery was amazing. Thirty days later, I was out of the hospital. Sixty days after my transplant I went back to work on light duty. The insurance that kicked in on the 365th day of my employment paid more than $2 million in hospital bills!

Several years have passed since my transplant. I am still sober and now weigh 225 pounds. The transformation God has made in my life is like night to day. I know that it is only by His grace and mercy that I am here today.

These days I try to show my gratitude to God by reaching out and helping others who are struggling with addictions. I have learned that no matter how far down the ladder someone has fallen, God still cares for them and wants to restore their life. Because of the transforming work God has done in my heart, I have reached out to the people I've harmed and to the employers I robbed, to make amends. Every debt I owed has now been paid.

In the most recent Christmas card my mother sent to me, she wrote, "… Ken, you've come a thousand miles!" Indeed, I have. I was a prisoner to my guilt, shame and addictions. Today I walk this earth a freed man—thanks be to God alone!

"He lifted me out of the slimy pit, out of the mud and mire; He set my feet on a rock and gave me a firm place to stand. He put a new song in my mouth, a hymn of praise to our God … Blessed is the man who makes the LORD his trust … "

- Psalm 40:2-4

—Ken Hinman, Florida

THE OAK TREE

After working a full day at the bank, I drove an hour and a half to attend a Bible study that evening. When the meeting was over two hours later, I headed out to make the hour and a half drive back to Mt. Pleasant.

Soon I began to feel extremely drowsy. To battle the sleepiness and stay awake, I did everything I could think of. I rolled the windows down for fresh air, turned the air conditioner on full blast, turned the radio way up and began singing along loudly. In the end, I lost the battle.

Suddenly my eyes popped open just in time to see my car heading for a big tree! There was no time to respond to what was happening. No time to jerk the car back on the road. All I could do in that moment was shout, "JESUS!"

My arms never moved, but, to my astonishment, something huge and white outside the front passenger side of my car effortlessly guided my car back onto the road! Everything happened in a flash. Yet to this day, when I close my eyes, I can still picture that angelic being. He was enormous—around eight feet tall—clothed in radiant white, and he had an unearthly brilliance.

The best part of this story is that before I invited Jesus into my heart and life, I used to contemplate ways to die, believing I had nothing to live for. Many times, I drove by that same oak tree and thought about driving my car into it. The fact that God chose that very spot to show me His love and protection, comforts me greatly.

This incident was a startling, but wonderful reminder that God has given me a purpose and hope worth living for!

—Nicola Soule, Michigan

THE RACE CAR

In 1986, my wife Lori and I bought a large, two-story farmhouse on the outskirts of Shepherd, Michigan. The hundred-plus year-old home was in need of a lot of work. At the time, I made good money working in the oil fields, but spent much of my time partying, drinking alcohol and doing drugs. There was never any extra money to do repairs or remodeling to the house.

In 1992, I stopped drinking and regularly attended meetings to keep sober, but still had a great deal of unrest in my life. Six months later, I invited the Lord into my heart and my life changed dramatically.

With drinking and drugs out of my life, there was finally some extra money that could be used to fix up the house. Instead, I approached my wife about investing a substantial amount of money into building a race car.

For years, I had gone to the race track on the weekends. Watching the drivers compete at the drag strip was something I truly enjoyed. I had a deep affection for speed and desired to own and drive my own race car. I had already bought a partially-assembled race car frame, but it would take close to $20,000 to build it into a car that could be raced at the track.

My idea did not go over too well with Lori. Every time I brought up the subject, a conflict arose. Putting money into house repairs and other necessities made a lot more sense to her than spending money on a race car.

In the summer of 1995, on a Saturday night, I went to the drag strip and, as usual, got fired up about working on the car. The following Sunday morning, as Lori and I were lying in bed talking, I brought up the topic again about building the race car. She was not responding real comfortably. I explained to Lori that I could sell a spare tractor I had, for two or three thousand dollars and put it toward the hot rod. Our conflict turned into a slightly heated argument.

At this time in my life, I had only been a Christian for a few years. But I had read my Bible and been around the church long enough to learn some things about faith and prayer. In 1 John 5:13-14 it says: "This is the confidence we have in approaching God: that if we ask anything according to his will, he hears us. And if we know that he hears us—whatever we ask—we know that we have what we asked of him." I knew that we could tell the Lord what was in our hearts, even our desires, and if it was within His will, He would give it to us. So I said to my wife, "Well, you're always telling me that we should bring everything before the Lord, so let's pray about this. Let's pray that if it's the Lord's will for me to fix up the car and get involved in racing, then let's ask Him to let the tractor sell."

Lori agreed, and we climbed out of bed and got down on our knees. I said a simple prayer: "Lord, if this would be something of Your will that I fix up the race car and pursue racing, then please let the tractor sell." We left it there in the Lord's hands.

Within ten minutes after our prayer, the phone rang. A fellow named Eddie wanted to know if I still had that tractor! I had mentioned to a few people that I had an extra tractor available to sell, but had never put up a For Sale sign anywhere. Eddie's brother-in-law was looking for a tractor and wanted to know if they could come over and look at it before Lori and I went to church.

Within a half hour the two men showed up. After driving the tractor around the driveway a bit, Eddie's brother-in-law asked me what I wanted for it. He bought it on the spot with cash without even trying to talk me down on the price. In less than an hour and a half after Lori and I prayed, the tractor was sold!

God made it clear to my wife and me that it was His will for me to start working on the race car. This really blessed me because it showed the Lord was listening to my prayers too, and that it was OK with Him to give me some of the desires of my heart.

The race car took four years to complete. We named it Divine Power, which we had painted on both sides of the car, along with a lightning bolt. We began racing the car at Mid Michigan Motorplex.

Oftentimes my wife and I had opportunities to share the Lord with people at the drag strip. I was not bothered a bit to be around the old drinking, partying atmosphere that used to be such a part of my life. Instead, I was filled with love for these guys and wanted to tell them about the love and hope the Lord had put in my heart. After a while, I was nicknamed "The Preacher." My wife Lori has a beautiful voice and often sang the anthem at the Northern National race meet openings.

Lori and I got involved with an organization called Racers for Christ—a group of Christian race car drivers who go to the national meets and hold worship services for the racers, their families, and anyone else willing to come. Lori was invited several times to sing at the chapel services.

Through the Racers for Christ outreach, we were invited to go to Ohio with our race car, where some world champions would be. Lori sang, and I spoke about some of the things the Lord has done in my life. That experience was a blessing I will never forget.

On many occasions, God used the race car to open other doors for us to tell others about the love of Jesus. One time we were invited to a camp for troubled youth. We took the race car, started it up for the kids and let them sit in it, then shared our testimony.

Months later, we received a letter from one of the boys who had been at the camp. He wanted us to know how much he appreciated us. He wrote: "I don't remember what you said, but my life has been changed." He went on to say he had made a decision to follow Christ, that life had new meaning for him now, and that he was happy.

In 1998, we started our own crane, transport, and millwright business that we also named Divine Power. The Lord has blessed us. And yes, we eventually did repairs and remodeling on our house. God has been good!

—Lonnie & Lori Brooks, Michigan

HOLY -IN- FILLING

When I was four months pregnant with my first child, I started having terrible pain in the right side of my mouth. My lower jaw and cheek area were even sore to the touch. Being blessed with good dental insurance, but fairly new to the area, I quickly made an appointment with a new dentist. Like many people, I'm a little squeamish in the dental chair, so when I saw the name Gentle Dental in the business pages, I decided that was the dentist for me—praying and hoping against false advertising!

The office staff was very friendly and made me feel right at home. When the dentist examined my teeth, he discovered a cavity. Then I was taken to a room where my mouth was X-rayed from several different angles. After studying my X-rays for some time, the dentist came into the room, sat down across from me and informed me that we had a dilemma. Although the cavity needed to be addressed soon, it was extremely close to a major nerve. The anesthesia necessary for the procedure posed risks for my unborn child. Basically, I was told to tough it out for the remainder of my pregnancy and was given a rescheduled appointment for after the baby's due date.

During the next few weeks the pain only worsened. Knowing I had nearly five months to go before it could be taken care of, I did a lot of praying and took lots of Tylenol!

About a month after the dental appointment, an evangelist visited the church I attended. After he finished speaking at the evening service, he told us that God wanted to heal people. He also told us we did not need to go up to the front for prayer, but that we could all just stay in our seats. I remember thinking, *Is this really going to work? Shouldn't we at least have to go up to the front of the church where the evangelist is? Wouldn't it be a more spiritual setting to be near the altar?*

Of course, after thinking about it, I knew that the evangelist did not have the ability to heal anyone, but that it was God who did the healing. Remembering some of the New Testament Bible stories, I recalled that Jesus most often healed people right where they were, whether it was on the streets or in their homes. It certainly would not be a problem for Him to heal someone who was still in their seat at church.

The evangelist began calling out specific maladies that he told us God wanted to heal. He instructed that those people who had these illnesses were to stand up and believe God for their healing. Then he said God wanted to heal those in need of dental work. That caught my attention! To those of us with a dental need, the evangelist told us to open our mouths and start believing God would heal us.

Although I felt a little funny standing there with my mouth gaped open, I felt honored that God wanted to heal me. Immediately I felt something happen. I knew the Great Physician had just touched me! From that moment on all the pain in my mouth was gone! Excitedly, I shared my testimony with my church family. Four months later, I gave birth to a beautiful baby boy.

The pain in my mouth had been long forgotten until the day I noticed the small white card hanging on the refrigerator with my rescheduled dental appointment, set for the following morning. Canceling the appointment at such late notice seemed inconsiderate, and I was curious about what had become of my cavity. Had God just made it vanish, or what? Knowing that this could be a great confirmation for my healing, I decided to go to my appointment.

At the dentist's office, the staff took more X-rays. The dentist looked shocked as he compared the before and after X-rays of my mouth. The more he looked at the X-rays, the more he shook his head in disbelief.

He commented that whoever filled my tooth was a highly skilled technician to pull off filling a cavity that posed such dire risks, due to its close location to the nerve. The dentist told me that if whoever drilled my tooth had been even slightly off, I would have been in excruciating pain. He wanted to know the name of the dentist who had filled my tooth while I was pregnant.

Happily, I told him that I had not been to another dentist while I was pregnant and that the Great Physician had filled my cavity! We both agreed that it had to have been a miracle. The proof was right before our eyes and, in my case, right inside my mouth!

—Nicole Nolley, Florida

THE BABY BLUE JAY

For a number of years I drove a school bus. Because I was allowed to keep my bus at home, I always backed it into our driveway. A large maple tree in our yard provided shade for the front end of it.

A two-week school spring break had just begun when a baby blue jay fell out of its nest and landed near the right front tire of my bus. The baby bird managed to wedge itself underneath the crevice of the tire for protection.

From the front window of our dining room, I would observe the mother blue jay come and feed her baby several times a day. She seemed to spend the remainder of her time camped out in the maple tree keeping a watchful eye for predators.

Blue jays can be extremely protective of their young. I learned that the hard way one day when I decided to take a closer look at the cute, little baby bird. It was my first and only experience of being dive-bombed by an upset bird. The mamma blue jay swooped down out of the tree and rammed me in the side of the head! After that, I decided not to go near the front of my bus or the tree.

Time passed quickly, and before I knew it, spring break was over. School would start the next morning and there was still a baby bird nestled under my front bus tire!

My friend Sarah dropped over for a visit late Sunday afternoon. We were having a cup of coffee when I happened to glance out the window and noticed the mother blue jay bringing food to her baby. Reminded of the dilemma I was in, I expressed my concerns to my friend. Having grown fond of the baby bird, I did not want to squash it Monday morning, nor did I want to be dive-bombed by an irate mother blue jay while performing my bus inspection.

My friend and I decided to pray about the situation and asked God to please have the baby blue jay change its location. We also asked God to heal any possible injuries the little bird may have sustained from the fall. Since my husband and I owned a dog and a couple of cats lived across the road, we concluded our prayer by asking God to keep the baby blue jay safe until it learned to fly.

When it was time for Sarah to go home, less than an hour after we prayed, I walked outside with her. To our amazement, the baby blue jay was now sitting on my front porch between two of the wooden spindles! The little bird had to hop all the way across the front yard and up three steps to get there! For the next couple of weeks the baby blue jay stayed on the front porch, until one day it just flew off.

God's love and care astounds me. There is nothing too big or too small to bring before the Lord in prayer—anything that concerns us, concerns Him!

"Are not five sparrows sold for two pennies? Yet not one of them is forgotten by God. Indeed, the very hairs of your head are all numbered. Don't be afraid; you are worth more than many sparrows."

- Luke 12:6-7

—Nina Stellwagen, Michigan

REVEALING X-RAY

I started drinking at a very young age. Having a beer or two at the tavern with my Dad before I was 10 years old was a common practice for me. My drinking only escalated through the years. By the age of 30, I was a full-blown alcoholic, drinking no less than a quart of vodka and an eight-pack of beer per day.

In April of 1987, at the age of 43, I gave my heart to the Lord. My baptism was scheduled for two weeks later.

The Sunday morning of my baptism, before going to church, I was fixing my usual breakfast—a vodka and orange juice, when an audible voice spoke to me about my drinking and let me know it was time to make a choice! Immediately I poured all my vodka and beer down the drain and managed to make it to church that morning to be baptized. I have heard stories where people were instantly delivered from alcohol and never experienced any withdrawal, but that was not my case. For five days straight I went through agony, breaking out in sweats, having the shakes or being sick. God blessed me with a wonderful wife who helped me through those days. After that first week and a lot of prayer, I was OK. For some reason I felt I needed to go through that time, but I also knew God was setting me free. In all my previous attempts to quit drinking, I had never succeeded.

In less than two weeks after I stopped drinking, I had major hip surgery. For some time I had been experiencing extreme pain in my hip. X-rays showed a cyst on the ball of my right hipbone that needed to be removed.

During my surgery, the physicians made an incision from my knee to hip joint. Then they cut completely through the thighbone about six inches above my knee and temporarily took out the bone to remove the cyst. Once finished, they put everything back together, using a steel plate with four screws to hold the reconnected bone in place. During my long, painful recovery, my wife Barb took care of me. My body took over seven months to heal enough for me to return to work.

At this time, I was still smoking three packs of cigarettes a day. Then, God spoke to me about my smoking. So, about a year after I had dumped my booze down the drain, I threw my cigarettes away. This turned out to be much harder than I thought it would be. After about a week of not smoking, I told the Lord, "If You don't do something, I'm going to wind up smoking again." All my former endeavors to stop smoking had failed. I knew I needed divine intervention or I was not going to make it this time. God heard my plea for help and strengthened me, enabling me to get through those tough times.

After I had been back to work for three and a half years, the pain in my hip returned. Going back to my doctor to have my hip rechecked, X-rays showed that the top third of the ball in my hip joint had crumbled, due to arthritis. I would need a hip replacement. Because of the pain and long healing time of the first surgery, I told the doctor that I wouldn't have it done until I absolutely had to have the surgery. He told me that if I waited any longer than six months, I would be crippled. I told everyone at work that I would need my hip replaced in six months. For the next three months I was in chronic pain.

One day Barb and I decided to attend a church service where an evangelist was speaking. In all honesty, it was the worst sermon I ever heard. Whatever the man was saying was not making any sense to me. Glancing around the room, I noticed puzzled looks on many faces.

When the sermon was over, the evangelist invited people to the altar for healing prayer. Still feeling slightly frustrated by the sermon, I did not want to go up there. But knowing the pain I had been in and knowing my need for an extra nudge, my wife said, "You can never get too much prayer." So I went up and stood in front of the farthest end of the altar. Setting my frustrations aside, I began talking with God, telling Him how much He meant to me, that He was everything I needed and so much more. Filled with gratefulness, I told Him that if I could have picked a God for myself, I could never have picked a God as great as He is!

God started blessing me so much with His love, I forgot that I was in church. Suddenly I became aware that the speaker was standing in front of me. He asked me what I needed prayer for. After I told him about my hip, he prayed for me. Then he told me that God was going to heal me, but that it would be day by day. I thanked him politely, but I didn't really believe him. On the way back to my seat, I noticed that the pain in my hip was gone! My pain had been 24/7, and now I was feeling fine. After two weeks I was still pain free, so I began telling everyone that God was healing me.

Soon the six months were up when I had tentatively planned to schedule my hip replacement. Knowing something had changed, I went back to my doctor for more X-rays, never dreaming of the big surprise in store for me. The X-rays no longer showed a crumbled hip joint, but revealed a brand new, healthy-looking bone! Instead of going into the hospital for a hip replacement, I went in as an outpatient, where the old plate and screws were removed in two hours' time. I was back to work in two weeks.

More than 18 years later, I am still alcohol free, and smoke free, have a pain-free hip, and I no longer limp! Thank you, Lord Jesus!

—George Pierce, Florida

HOW LOVELY

NOTE FROM THE EDITOR: The name of the man referred to as "William" in this story was changed to protect his privacy.

Numerous times in my life, I have witnessed how great God's love is towards all people—pursuing them right to the very end of their lives. One of these occasions happened several years ago while I was the pastor of Coldwater Assembly of God Church.

At the time, I was blessed to have a secretary named Mary. At 76 years of age, she continued to lead relatives and friends to Christ. One of these people was a man named William. On a few occasions, William's mother also came to church. However, she had never made any personal commitment to follow Christ.

One night William called me on the phone and said, "Pastor, my mother is dying. Would you come and pray with her?" I headed for the hospital as soon as I could.

William was waiting for me when I entered his mother's hospital room. Immediately, I noticed a woman I did not know sitting in a chair. She had a notably unwelcome, mad expression on her face.

Out of her earshot, I asked William, "Who is she?"

He said, "She's my sister-in-law and she's an atheist. She doesn't want you preaching or talking to my mom about the Lord at all!"

I walked over to the bed, noticing William's mother was curled up in the fetal position with her legs drawn up to her chest. She was in a coma.

Before I had time to start praying, William's sister-in-law looked over at me with a scowl on her face and blurted out, "We don't need any religion now. Imagine, bringing religion into a situation like this!" Disturbed, I turned around and walked out of the room. William followed me and said, "Pastor, you've got to pray with my mom!"

Knowing it would be difficult to contend with his sister in-law, I said, "I'll tell you what we'll do. We'll pray and ask the Lord to keep your mom in the exact same position she's in until I can get back and pray with her."

The next day I called William and asked him if there would be a time when no one else would be in his mother's room. He told me people were there all day except from 12:00 to 1:00 p.m., when everyone went to lunch.

Thursday morning a pastor stopped by my house to see me. We visited for a while. But as the time got closer to 12:00 p.m., I asked him if he wanted to go along with me to make a hospital call, which he agreed to do. On the way, I told him we would be praying with a woman who was in a coma.

Surprised, he responded, "She's in a coma!?" I reassured him, feeling confident that a coma would not be an obstacle for God.

We walked into the hospital room, and William's mom was lying in the exact fetal position she was in Monday night when I last saw her. Standing by her bed, I spoke to William's mother in faith, believing she would be able to hear me, and told her another pastor and I were there to pray with her.

She immediately sat up in bed, and said, "Well, how lovely of you to come." The other pastor standing at the foot of her bed almost fell over in surprise. But I wasn't surprised; I was expecting it. Faith builds on faith, and I had witnessed God's power many times in my life.

Looking at William's mother, I said, "You've been to church a few times. You need the Lord. Why don't I pray with you, and you accept the Lord into your heart?"

She replied, "How lovely." The other pastor read Psalm 91. Then I led William's mother in a prayer where she invited Jesus to come into her heart.

Afterward, I told her I would be back the next day to see how she was doing and bring her some literature, and then we left. William's mom went right back into her coma, pulled up tight in the fetal position and died shortly after.

That same afternoon William called me on the phone, very upset. "My mother died without the Lord!" he said.

"William—no, she didn't," I responded. When I got to tell William what had happened, he was overjoyed!

"The Lord is not slow in keeping His promise, as some understand slowness. He is patient with you, not wanting anyone to perish, but everyone to come to repentance."

- 2 Peter 3:9

—Charles Booth, Michigan

DIVINE RESCUE

It was a cool brisk morning, and my husband Que and I were still in bed. Our little dog began acting sick and wanted to go outside. When I got out of bed to let the dog out, my head began to pound like a drum so hard that I thought I was having a heart attack!

Once the dog was out, I quickly laid down on the couch. Feeling too ill to move, I soon called to my husband and told him to let our little dog back in. When he got out of bed, his head and heart began to pound too! After letting our dog in, Que went straight back to bed. We were both feeling so terrible that neither one of us wanted to budge.

I was still lying on the couch when all at once a commanding, audible voice said to me, "Get out of the house now!" Looking around, I could see no one there!

Startled, I yelled to my husband and said, "We've got to get out of here right now!"

He called back, "I'm not moving."

Again the audible voice spoke—this time with even greater urgency: "Get out of the house now!"

Managing somehow to get up, I went into the bedroom and said to my husband, "Come on! You're getting out of here if I have to drag you!"

We got the dog and went out to the screened-in patio. Our neighbor lady noticed that something seemed to be wrong and came right over to help us. Our heads and hearts were still pounding so hard we thought they would explode!

Once in the fresh air, we soon began feeling better and quickly called a family friend who worked with blast furnaces. He came right over and tested our house for carbon monoxide. The levels were so high that he told us if we had not gotten out of the house when we did, we would have soon died!

During the evening before, my husband Que installed two new motors in our furnace. As it turned out, the motors were too big. When we turned on the furnace in the morning to take the chill off the house, the oversized fans caused carbon monoxide to back up into the house.

That we ever left the house that morning is a wonder. Not only were we both so sick that neither one of us wanted to move, but we were unable to rationalize clearly. If it had not been for the urgent warning from that audible voice, we would have never left the house.

God had His angels watching over us. We were saved by His divine power!

—Olive Waltz, Florida

PEACE IN THE PAIN

"The righteous perish, and no one ponders it in his heart; devout men are taken away, and no one understands that the righteous are taken away to be spared from evil." -Isaiah 57:1

In 1963, my husband Dean and I were blessed with our second child, a baby girl. Dawn was born three weeks early and weighed a mere four pounds and 14 ounces. We brought her home from the hospital two weeks later. Dawn Yvonne Miller had a special destiny. God had an awesome plan for this tiny, little one.

At Dawn's six weeks checkup, our family physician noticed a heart murmur. He set up an appointment for Dawn to see a cardiologist at Ford Hospital in Detroit. After the cardiologist examined her and ran multiple tests, he informed us that our daughter had a boot-shaped, single chamber heart with numerous defects. He also told us Dawn's future was very bleak, offering us little hope. Later, we met with Dr. Edward Green, Chief of Pediatric Cardiology, who gave us some hope that future surgeries might help Dawn.

Dawn's heartbeat was extremely rapid. You could see her heartbeat through her clothing and blankets. On a good day, she was blue. When she had a cardiac episode, she would turn nearly black.

One day while my husband Dean was at work, Dawn's heart quit! Our two-year-old son Glen and Dawn were down for a nap. Although no TV, radio or noise of any kind was going on, I suddenly felt something was very wrong. Fear clutched at my heart. I did not want to go into the nursery, but I felt like someone was literally pushing me!

Upon entering the room, I knew Dawn was gone. In a panicked frenzy I did everything wrong—I started screaming her name, hit her chest and shook her! I remember saying, "You will not die! I won't let you!" Then I took Dawn into the living room, laid her on the sofa, and began giving her mouth-to-mouth resuscitation. Between breaths I would call out, "Oh God, please help me!" After a few of my faltering attempts, Dawn started breathing.

After this frightening episode my husband and I took Dawn to Ford Hospital. They did multiple tests and kept her overnight. We were not given much hope, but the cardiologist discussed possibly having a Blalock shunt performed on Dawn. If the surgery was a success, more oxygen would be delivered to her blood, which would significantly improve her quality of life. However, we were told her chances of surviving the surgery were between nil and nothing. Since this wasn't any less hope than we had already been given, we elected to have the surgery. Prayer changes things, because to everyone's amazement eight-month-old Dawn came through the surgery with flying colors.

From the time Dawn was three she started talking about going home to be with Jesus. She would get up in the morning and say, "I thought Jesus was going to come and take me home last night. Oh well, maybe tonight." This was very upsetting to me. We were trying so hard to keep her alive, yet she wanted to go "home" and live with Jesus!

As the years passed Dawn endured many dark days, but she always told everyone how much God loved them and what Jesus had done for them on the cross. She would urge friends as well as other patients in the hospital to invite Jesus into their hearts. Dawn frequently read her Bible and asked questions. She glowed with a special radiance that those who are very close to the Lord have. People noticed. Again and again, people would tell me, "The whole room lights up when she walks in."

After Dawn, we had three more children: Tara, Nicole and Danae. Our fourth child Danae was born with a "simple" cardiac problem. An obstruction just above one of her heart valves was like a flipper. At times, this flipper would flop over the valve, and Danae would turn blue and lose consciousness. Doctors could perform a simple surgery to correct this problem, but preferred to wait until she was a little older to do the procedure.

Danae responded well to medications for a while, but continued having cardiac episodes. By the time she was 12 months old she was having them daily, so we moved her crib into the living room. Every time she had an episode, we would set her on our lap and hold an oxygen mask over her mouth. Eventually, Danae would take the oxygen mask from us and hold it over her own mouth. When the episode was over, she would hand it back and say, "All done." Then she would sleep for a while.

Danae was just short of 16 months old when the doctors decided it was time for her surgery. We were assured that after this simple procedure, she would be 100 percent normal. Instead, she slipped into a coma and suffered irreversible brain damage. Danae lingered on machines for 10 days, then went home to be with the Lord.

On the way home from Ford Hospital, our best friends traveled in the car with us. Yet I was in such shock over losing Danae that I was not even aware that people were talking to me. My pain and sorrow were so great that I felt I would never be able to function again, let alone take care of the other children at home.

Then an amazing thing happened. Once we arrived home, God poured out His supernatural peace over me! The ride home seemed to be a demonstration of the pain I would be experiencing if I bore this terrible loss on my own. I still felt the loss, but somehow God's sweet peace seemed to hover over me. He gave me "peace that passes all understanding" (Philippians 4:7). There was a knowing within me, that if I did not have the Lord to turn to, this would be unbearable.

Every day I would relinquish my pain to the Lord, and each day He would strengthen and sustain me with His loving peace and comfort. It enabled me to take care of the other children, and every day I grew stronger.

Dawn absolutely adored Danae and had been like a second

mother to her. As we expected, she took Danae's passing very hard. Dawn was 11 years old at the time and knew that, in the not-too-distant future, she would be having her own open-heart surgery.

Although the Blalock shunt performed on Dawn at eight months old had lasted several years, her health was now seriously declining.

Dealing with congestive heart failure and poor circulation, she was very thin and cold all the time. Her liver, spleen and heart were so enlarged that her abdomen was swollen. For the next five years, while all her classmates were maturing, Dawn stayed the same size.

The time came when Dawn convinced Dr. Green that she could take no more. She struggled to get oxygen whenever she lay down. When she tried to sleep sitting up, she would awake numerous times throughout the night. She was suffering in many other ways, too. Her cardiologist knew that neither Dawn, nor her heart, could endure much more.

Dr. Green contacted associates at Mayo Clinic who told him that the best surgeon for the job was right there at the Children's Hospital in Detroit, where we had transferred Dawn after Danae's passing. The prospective surgeon whom Dr. Green had contacted, did not want to do the surgery.

This surgeon was very skilled and a wonderful, kind and caring man who loved children. Whenever he came across children he could not help or, worse yet, if he lost one, he became heartbroken.

The surgery proposed for Dawn had incredible risks and the chances of her survival were slim. The plan was to rebuild her heart by creating an artificial wall made of raincoat-type material that would give her heart a second chamber. If the operation worked, it could transform Dawn's life. However, this type of surgery was still in its pioneer stages, and the surgeon had never performed it before. Attempting such a risky procedure for the first time on a sixteen-year-old girl seemed inconceivable to him.

Since no other options were left that had the potential to help

Dawn, Dr. Green had a talk with the surgeon. Being a little tough with him, he said, "Go talk to that little girl and tell her why you won't try to help her."

The surgeon went in to talk to Dawn and told her he did not think she realized how dangerous this operation was. Dawn's response to him was something like this: "Every time they've operated on me, they've told my parents I didn't have a chance, but God helped me make it through. I trust in God, and I trust in Jesus and I trust in you. Do you know my Jesus? And besides, if I don't make it, that's OK, too. I've wanted to be with Jesus since I was three years old, and I miss my baby sister."

The surgeon smiled at her and said, "You can tell your parents that I'm willing to try to help you. I will do the surgery."

On the first day of spring in 1979, Dawn had her surgery. The operating room was filled with numerous medical staff and students who would be observing this attempt to create an artificial heart wall. The surgery went very well and appeared to be a huge success. Dawn came off the heart and lung machine just fine. Everyone was ecstatic—and then Dawn started hemorrhaging.

At the beginning of her surgery, numerous adhesions were removed that had built up during the sixteen years Dawn's heart had worked so hard. Her body hemorrhaged through these areas.

The medical staff worked desperately to save her, but to no avail. Free at last, Dawn went to sleep and quietly slipped away to Jesus. The surgeon was heartbroken, breaking into sobs as he gave us the news.

Once again, in the midst of my pain, God poured His supernatural peace into me. Without His precious comfort, I knew this would be a burden too great for me to bear. Only God was able to fill that place in my heart with His unexplainable peace.

God knows just what each one of us needs. Our youngest daughter Nicole was four years old when Dawn died, and she spent many years not understanding why God would allow her sister to be taken away. In His perfect timing, God had a special appointment planned for Nicole.

Twenty-five years later Nicole went to her insurance agency to take care of some business. Her usual agent was not there that day. Nicole was not thrilled with the idea of dealing with an unfamiliar agent, but rather than make another trip to the agency, she agreed to talk to a different person.

The insurance agent directed to help Nicole was named Michelle, who had a picture of her three children displayed in her office. When Nicole remarked about the picture, Michelle began telling Nicole about her little boy. He had been born with a boot-shaped heart with only one chamber. At a very young age, he had a major heart surgery where an artificial heart wall was created to give his heart a second chamber. He had started kindergarten with the rest of the kids his age and was now living a normal life.

Nicole, filled with emotion, shared the story about her sister Dawn going through the same surgery 25 years earlier, when very little was known about what was at that time considered an extremely risky operation. Although Dawn had lost her battle during the surgery, a monumental discovery was made in the process. The surgery itself was found to be a complete success, but doctors realized that the surgery needed to be performed on those with this heart defect at a very early age, before adhesions began to develop.

Soon Michelle and Nicole were both in tears. Joy began to flood Nicole's heart. Until that very moment, she had not understood that what was learned through Dawn's surgery was now bringing life and hope to others! She could not help but wonder how many other children's lives had been changed or saved since that day when Dawn's earthly life ended—perhaps thousands around the world! How many tears had been spared? The much-needed healing, understanding, and complete closure over Dawn's death was given to Nicole that day. Her sadness turned to jubilant happiness! Nicole's realization brought much joy to my husband and me, as well.

Before going in for her final surgery, Dawn had said to me, "I always wanted to be a missionary." I told her she already had been one all her life. Then she told me, "I wanted to do something special for people with my life." At that time, I could only tell her how much she meant to us. Little did Dawn know that her last desire would become a reality!

Life can be very hard sometimes. But our family has learned to put our trust in God. The Bible says, "Trust in the Lord with all your heart and lean not on your own understanding" (Proverbs 3:5) and "We know that in all things God works for the good of those who love Him, who have been called according to His purpose" (Romans 8:28). Sometimes it is impossible to see the good in a difficult situation, and we will have to wait until we are home with the Lord before we know the reasons why some things happen.

Our family has come to learn that God pours out His peace and strength richly just when we need it. We are comforted to know that the separation from our girls is temporary. And we look forward to that grand reunion when we will all be "Home" at last!

—Diana Miller, Michigan

BOILING OIL

One evening when the kids were younger, I experienced a bizarre miracle while cooking supper. As is typical with many moms, fixing supper is often hectic, juggling three or four tasks at one time. In addition to preparing a couple side dishes, I was in the process of deep-frying a big batch of fish. A plate of cod fillets and bowl of batter were conveniently positioned to the left of a six-quart deep fryer.

After frying fish for about twenty minutes, I was about to dip one of the few remaining fillets into the dwindling batter, when I was suddenly distracted by one of the kids. In a hurried, thoughtless moment, I turned my body slightly to the right to see what was going on, when my hand plunged down into the boiling oil instead of the batter!

My initial reaction was to rush to the sink and run cold water over my hand. Before I even reached the faucet, I realized I was not feeling any pain whatsoever! Then it began to register—the oil had only felt lukewarm and bubbly when my hand went down into it! Right before my eyes, I could see golden brown fish still sizzling in the boiling oil. My hand had not even turned pink. It was only covered with oil that I simply needed to wash off! Without a doubt, I knew I had experienced a miracle.

Several years earlier, while cooking for a fund-raising dinner, I was removing a country-fried steak from a large deep fryer, when boiling oil ran down the handle of the spoon and onto my hand. The second-degree burns took weeks to heal.

My peculiar miracle brought to mind a story I had read in *Foxe's Book of Martyrs*. Not far into the book was an account of the attempt to martyr the Apostle John, one of Jesus' disciples, who also penned the book of Revelation. According to *Foxe's Book of Martyrs*, Emperor Domitian had ordered John to be boiled in a cauldron of oil, but it was reported that a miracle occurred and the boiling oil did not harm him.

After having immersed my hand in boiling oil with no ill effects whatsoever, the story newly intrigued me. With a big smile on my face, I could not help but wonder if the apostle John experienced what it would feel like to be tossed into a Jacuzzi filled with warm, bubbling oil! Obviously, he must have marveled over his situation with far greater appreciation than I felt for mine.

God demonstrated to me that He is well able to deliver us from undesirable experiences. However, I have also learned from the past, this is not the case much of the time. Somehow, my strange miracle left me with a peace-filled assurance that regardless of what the future holds—we can trust God with every step of the journey!

"Have I not commanded you? Be strong and courageous. Do not be terrified; do not be discouraged, for the Lord your God will be with you wherever you go."
  - Joshua 1:9

—Nina Stellwagen, Michigan

THE EARRING

My son Bond was eight years old when he was diagnosed with acute lymphomatic leukemia. For the next several years he was in and out of hospitals going through treatments or tests. Other times he was busy being a typical boy, hanging out with his friends and having fun.

One day when Bond was undergoing one of his treatments at Mott Children's Hospital in Ann Arbor, Michigan, a man and woman came into his room. They were at the hospital visiting someone else when they heard there was a teenage boy in a nearby room that had leukemia. This couple owned a dude ranch in Steamboat, Colorado that featured white-water rafting, horseback riding, hiking and other family-friendly fun. They floored us when they said they would like to send Bond and any of our immediate family members on an all-expenses-paid trip to their ranch!

In the summer of 1999, at age fourteen, Bond, along with my husband and our two youngest daughters, boarded an airplane and headed for the Vista Verde Ranch. While my two oldest daughters and I attended other important events already on the calendar, the rest of my family spent a memorable week at the ranch.

When Bond returned home, he surprised me with a present. Because he knew I loved hearts, he had picked out a pair of post-style earrings that had a gold heart suspended beneath a small blue stone. The warm smile on his face when he gave me the earrings and saw how much I loved them was a priceless moment. I knew I would always treasure those earrings!

One night, after wearing the earrings only a few times, I was taking off one of the earrings by pulling the back off, when the front part of it flipped off, flew through the air and fell down into an air-conditioning vent. I felt terribly upset! Thinking that someday we would go through the process of trying to retrieve it, I put the remaining earring back in its box and set it on the nightstand by my bed.

Nearly four years later in November of 2003, at age seventeen, Bond went home to be with the Lord. The grieving process was painful and difficult. Doing basic household duties and being a mom to my remaining four daughters took everything I had in me. In-depth cleaning projects requiring concentration were put on hold.

Three years after Bond's death, I finally felt strong enough to do some of the deep-cleaning jobs I had put off. One of the tasks I decided to do was sort through everything on the nightstand, which had become a catchall for books, letters and cards.

As the pile of clutter dwindled down, I uncovered the earring box. I had forgotten about those earrings that Bond had so lovingly picked out just for me. Upon opening the box and seeing the single remaining earring, I burst into tears and cried inconsolably.

That night I went to bed, still grieving deeply. My heart ached so much from missing Bond that it was almost more than I could endure. Although I knew Bond was with the Lord and that heaven had to be a remarkable place—it just seemed so far away. I longed to see Bond and for assurance that he really was OK and happy. I began crying out to God, "Lord, please let me hear from Bond! Please give me some kind of a sign that he's doing OK!" Eventually, completely exhausted, I fell asleep.

During the night I had the most vivid dream that Bond came to see me. He looked marvelous and so happy. He stood before me holding my missing earring, then he handed it to me! One would think I would be most elated to see my son, and I was overjoyed to see him. But, strangely, in my dream my greatest excitement seemed to be that he had found my other earring. I excitedly exclaimed to him, "Bond! You found my earring!" With a warm grin covering his handsome face, he simply replied, "No problem!" I felt happy beyond measure; then the dream was over.

The moment I woke up the following morning, my dream flooded back into my thoughts. I was lying in bed soaking up the joy the dream had given me, when something blue and gold caught my eye. My heart began pounding; the earring was laying on the nightstand! I clearly remembered that the earring had been in the box the night before. My thoughts raced, trying to rationalize what had happened. Did one of the girls take the earring out of the box and leave it on the nightstand after I fell asleep?

Shaking uncontrollably, I grabbed the small box and opened it—the other earring was inside! I started screaming, "My earring! Bond! My earring!" I screamed so loud that one of the girls came running into the bedroom to see what was wrong. I was in such shock and so elated with joy that I was barely able to talk.

Later, of course, I questioned the whole family about retrieving the missing earring without my knowing it. They all assured me they had not and rejoiced with me.

Did Jesus come into my room and place the earring on the nightstand? Or an angel? Did God let Bond step out of heaven for one brief moment to place the earring there personally? I may never know the answers in this life.

What I do know is that God heard my cry and responded in a far more wonderful and comforting way than I could have ever imagined. This miracle brought me indescribable happiness and peace. What an added blessing to be able to wear those precious earrings again after nearly seven years.

I will never stop missing Bond or longing to see him. But, every time I see the two earrings together, I will be reminded of God's miraculous confirmation that Bond is alive, well and happy—and we will see him again someday in that Celestial City!

—Chris Marshall, California

NOTE FROM THE EDITOR: Prior to moving to California, Chris was a secretary for a non-profit establishment in Michigan, where I would see her one day each week. I will never forget the day in Chris' office as she excitedly told me about her miracle, only days after it happened. Sheer joy covered her face—especially as she turned her head from side to side for me to see both of those cherished earrings!

SURPRISE HARVEST

During the late 1930s, our family lived in the small town of Twin Lake, Michigan. We were a very poor family with eight children ranging in age from three to nineteen. I was around ten years old at the time.

Because of the 1929 stock market crash, many families struggled with financial hardships, and jobs were scarce. A war injury, plus a later serious hip injury, left my dad crippled, unable to get a job anywhere. He repaired bicycles; Mom took in ironing and whatever housecleaning jobs she could get. In the summertime, all of us kids would dig worms, which we sold to the local fishermen in order to help feed and clothe all of us. Making ends meet was always a challenge.

Having food for winter always presented added difficulties, but I don't ever remember worrying about it. Our mom always prayed that God would provide for us and taught us to do the same. Mom's faith was unwavering; she trusted God for everything. Whenever a situation looked bleak and Mom truly did not know what to do, she would always say, "We'll just put this in the Lord's hands!" Mom had total confidence that God would take care of us, and she always thanked Him in advance.

One fall Saturday afternoon while the weather was still nice, we older kids begged our parents to let us go on a hike with some neighbor kids. My brothers wanted to hunt for arrowheads, so about twelve of us in all started out on new territory, through woods and open fields and more woods. After wandering around for about three hours, the neighbor boys who thought they knew the way, admitted they were lost.

We were all tired, thirsty and hungry, and had no clue how to get back home. Then the boys spotted a small cabin in a clearing. We figured there would be a road from the cabin that would lead out to a main road, enabling us to find our way home.

When we got to the cabin it was locked, but there was a note on the door, which read:

*I had to leave in an emergency and
won't be back until spring. Anyone who might
find this note may help themselves to all the
produce in the garden and to the apples
and nuts in the orchard.*

We looked out on the other side of the cabin and saw that the garden was massive! It covered an area about two blocks long by two blocks wide. The garden was loaded with every kind of vegetable imaginable, and even some spices. We all ate some tomatoes right then and there. Soon after, we thought we had better follow the narrow dirt drive out to the main road, so we could get home and tell our folks about our wonderful find.

When we arrived home, our parents were upset because we were so late. Then we told them about the garden. They thought it seemed too good to be true and wanted to see for themselves. After checking it out, they got excited, too.

For the next week, our Dad, with the help of a neighbor man and his pickup truck, took all of us back there to gather the produce—we brought load after load home. After that, we made periodic trips to the garden and orchard and continued to gather the harvest until the snow fell. Mom canned up hundreds of quarts of tomatoes and other fruits and vegetables. We also loaded up the basement with potatoes, carrots, onions and apples. With dill weed and pickles (cucumbers) growing in the garden, we were able to make a huge barrel of dill pickles. Even popcorn was growing in the garden, which my Uncle Ed hung up to dry for us. What a treat! The abundance of produce provided numerous families with food for the entire winter. What a wonderful godsend! That turned out to be one of the best winters for our family and for several neighbors, too.

In the spring, our family went to thank the man who lived in the cabin. We found out he had been growing produce to sell at a farmer's market. When his brother became seriously ill, the man went to stay with him. The man was overjoyed to find out his garden had provided food for so many families in need.

Looking back years later, I realize how incredible the whole situation actually was. We kids had never gotten lost before, yet we managed to wander nearly four miles from home, in precisely the right direction to stumble across a huge abandoned garden exactly at harvest time!

Not only that, when us kids followed the long, obscure, two-track dirt drive that led away from the cabin out to the main road, the cabin was no longer in sight. There is no way someone traveling on the public road could have seen the cabin or garden. God undoubtedly led us to that abundance of produce!

God provided above and beyond what we even thought to ask for. What a blessing and lots of good eating too! One of Mom's favorite verses was:

"I was young and now I am old, yet I have never seen the righteous forsaken or their children begging bread."
- *Psalm 37:25*

—Dolly Straley, Florida

QUICK ANSWER TO PRAYER

Often throughout my day when my thoughts are free to talk to God—I do just that. It is a comfort to know that God is always there to listen.

One afternoon while volunteering at a Christ-centered pregnancy center, I was in deep thought about my 20-year-old daughter. Soon she would be moving to Missoula, Montana to attend the University of Montana. Missoula is a large city, and my husband and I did not know anyone who could answer our many questions about this college town. We were concerned about our daughter's safety. We had no idea what parts of the city might not be good to live in or the best housing prices in the safest areas. Another disheartening thought was that our daughter would not know anyone in Missoula. She would be such a long way from her home in Michigan.

I was washing up a small batch of dishes at the center while these thoughts were weighing on my mind. So I said a simple prayer: "Oh Lord, please put someone before me who has lived in Missoula, or knows someone who lives there, so we can learn more about the city and be guided in this process." I finished washing the dishes, gathered up a few pop cans, then headed out the door and across the parking lot to the 7- Eleven convenience store to return the soda cans.

Standing in front of the store were two old friends of my daughter. The three of us chatted a bit. Then I mentioned that my daughter was going to attend the University of Montana in Missoula. One of the girls exclaimed, "Missoula! That's where my sister lives!" I could hardly believe it! Talk about a quick answer to prayer! For the rest of the afternoon, I could not wipe the smile off my face.

A week later, after a few phone calls, my daughter was able to go and spend two days with her friend's sister and husband in Missoula. There she was given a tour of the city and received valuable information about housing and other important aspects concerning Missoula. She was also introduced to some of their friends. Now she would know some people when she went back to Missoula to stay.

I was so happy that God answered my prayer so quickly—only minutes after I prayed! I felt even more assured and thankful that God cares about the details of our lives.

—Sharon, Michigan

SCHOOL OF FAITH

For years, God had placed a thought in my heart to open a school for drug addicts, prostitutes, those who had been formerly incarcerated, the homeless and unloved. Part of me did not want to do this, because I felt completely inadequate. But God dearly loves these people, and He put a love and desire in my heart that would not go away to help them. My vision for the school was to offer rehabilitation to these precious people, while teaching them about the love of God.

After much prayer, I decided to take on this challenge of starting the school. I began contacting people I deemed as most qualified and having the best credentials to be in on the project. When we held meetings to discuss plans, I began to experience a feeling of discomfort—a "still, small inner voice" that implied something was not right—but I ignored it.

After all my planning and hard work, it looked as though the school would soon become a reality, when suddenly all my plans fell through the floor. I was devastated. For three months I felt as if I were on God's threshing floor. During this time I spent numerous, inconsolable hours weeping and crying out to God, but He remained silent.

One day I was praying when I heard God call my name: "Janet." The voice sounded like the voice of a loving father, gentle and soothing.

Then God called my name again: "Janet."

This time I said, "Here I am, Lord."

He said to me, "Do you know why you failed?"

I said, "No, I don't know."

He said, "You depended upon man. Now I want you to depend on Me, and I will show you my power!"

A huge burden lifted off me, and I said, "Thank you, Lord!" All of the emotional pain and sorrow I had been experiencing melted away.

Soon I got up and went into the kitchen. While I washed dishes, God spoke to me again and told me to call a prominent woman that I knew. She was a wonderful woman of God who has touched many peoples' lives; she also owned an office building. The thought entered my mind that perhaps this woman would have a space in which I could teach a class.

During our phone conversation, I asked the woman if she had a spare room that I could use for a classroom.

She said, "Janet, I have a whole building, and it's yours if you want it." How wonderful God is! I asked for a small space, and He gave me an entire building! Not only did it have a classroom, but three offices, a conference room, four bathrooms and storage space. The building needed some work and cleaning up, but in the year 2000, Corner Stone Faith Services opened its doors.

One day the school appeared to be in financial trouble. The school's funding came from donations and some government grants. We truly had to operate by faith! After I carefully made a list of all the expenses that needed to be paid that day, the total came to exactly $1,000—money I did not have, nor could think of where to get it.

Not knowing what else to do, I said a simple earnest prayer: "Lord, I need a thousand dollars!" After praying, I thanked Him in advance and went back to doing my usual tasks.

Around an hour later, a lady came to the school that sometimes brought food for the students. She handed an envelope to me and said, "I normally give this to another organization, but the Lord told me to give it to you."

Politely, I thanked her and took the envelope. Although I was very grateful for whatever donation she had made, I did not look to see how much it was. Because the woman appeared no better off than some of the students, I assumed her donation would be rather meager—at least not enough to take care of the dilemma we were in.

Later on that day, the Lord spoke to me and said, "Open up the envelope." So I opened it, and enclosed was a check for a thousand dollars!

What a marvelous God we have! He sent someone right to our doorstep—only one hour after the request was made—with the exact amount of money needed to supply our urgent need!

The school has been privileged to serve more than five hundred of God's special, valued people. He has provided our every need. Thank you, Lord!

"But my God shall supply all your need according to His riches in glory by Christ Jesus."

- Philippians 4:19 KJV

—Janet Matier, Michigan

IT'S LUNCH TIME

After four years of marriage, my husband and I purchased four acres of land that was part of a 40-acre tract of woods. We cleared hundreds of trees off our property and built our dream house, knowing it would be a wonderful place to raise a family. The Lord blessed us with four children in just four years!

When the kids were young, we spent a great deal of time working at making our backyard a fun place for all. We dug a pond, built a swing set with a fort on top, made a sandbox and a basketball area. In addition to this, the owner of the acreage surrounding our property gave us permission to hike and make forts in the woods. It was a child's paradise.

Many children, ranging in ages from five to twelve, made their way over to our place nearly every day to play with our kids. We enjoyed having them over and did not worry when they played outside. We had strict rules about staying away from the pond, and how far the kids were allowed to go into the woods unless an adult was with them. They were good kids who gladly obeyed our rules.

One morning several children were over playing outside, when our six-year-old daughter came running into the house, looking terrified. All the color had drained from her face. Instantly, I knew something was terribly wrong. At that moment, God filled me with an extraordinary sense of peace that enabled me to keep my composure. In my heart, I knew it was important for my daughter's sake that I remain calm.

In a gentle voice I asked her what was wrong. She said, "Nothing." I said, "I know something is wrong, honey. You need to tell mommy what it is." She began to whimper, "I'm not supposed to tell," but soon the story unfolded:

The kids had decided to play hide and seek in the woods. Seemingly, out of nowhere, a full-grown, young man appeared—a stranger to the children. He asked the kids if he could play hide and seek with them. The kids told him he could. This young man then said to our daughter, "Will you hide with me?" Feeling uneasy about hiding alone with him, she told him that they should each go hide on their own. But he played on her sympathy by acting sad and telling her he didn't know anyone and did not know his way around in the woods. After his persuasions, our daughter reluctantly and innocently went with him into the woods. Soon he began making advances that frightened her. She tried to convince him that they should go back to where the other kids were. Nothing she said convinced him to let her go, until . . .

Safely in our house, but still crying, she told me, "It's a good thing you called me to lunch!" To which I responded, "I never called you to lunch." She said, "Yes, you did! I heard you! You called me two times. It was your voice! Anyway, I told that guy that you would get really upset if I didn't come home for lunch right away, and you'd come looking for me! He told me not to tell what he did and took off."

My husband and I called the police, and the young man was later apprehended. After questioning all of the kids that were playing hide and seek that day, we learned that not one other child heard anyone call them to lunch. That did not surprise me, considering it was only about 10:00 a.m. when the incident happened, and I knew I had not called anyone to lunch!

Nearly three decades later, my daughter clearly recalls saying a prayer in the woods that morning: *Please God, let somebody find us!* Immediately, she heard the audible voice that sounded exactly like mine calling her to come home for lunch. She has no doubt that it was an angel.

My daughter's episode left her with a sensitivity towards others' hurts and issues. Throughout the years, God has opened up numerous opportunities for her to encourage and counsel such girls. We can now clearly see that what the enemy meant for evil, God has turned around and used for His glory!

—M. A., Michigan

GETTING INTO HOT WATER

I dreaded stripping down in front of villagers and being boiled like a lobster.

Since the moment our missionary team had agreed to help out with a gospel meeting in a southern coastal city on Honshu Island, Japan, I had worried obsessively. The meeting would be held during the hottest part of the summer, and I would have to use a neighborhood public bathhouse while we were there.

I was only 23—a modest, compliant, newly-wedded young woman from Michigan who, in the early 1970s, had been recruited right out of college alongside my young husband to teach English in Japan. During the day, we taught at a four-school campus; at night we held Bible studies in our home, which was also on campus. Our Western-style house provided—among other cultural luxuries—bathroom privacy, which had given me a level of comfort in an otherwise unfamiliar culture.

A sick feeling pervaded the pit of my stomach about using a public bath, even after all the praying. My first concern was having to undress in front of all the town women who would also be using the ofuro, their word for "bath." My fair skin, blonde hair and European features had drawn attention in Japan from day one. Everywhere I went, people stared. At first I enjoyed this movie star treatment. But by the end of six months, I longed for an anonymity that was not possible in a country where I stood out like a white dot on a black domino. I had no doubt that when I bathed at the ofuro, everyone would stare.

But the second issue was pure fear of the hot bath water. My calves were nearly scalded once at a quaint little inn in Nara. Another time when I was a guest in a Japanese home, my hosts graciously gave me "first dip" rights, before everyone else in the family took turns using the same water for soaking. They poured my bath water in a kind of barrel-shaped tub and then left the room. I tried, but I couldn't sit longer than a minute in that ofuro before I felt like screaming. It wasn't just me having a low tolerance for hot water. Japanese newspaper articles were reporting that the commonly extreme *ofuro* temperatures were lowering men's sperm counts!

Imagining myself at the upcoming public bath, I pictured a crowd of native women watching me step down into the large in-ground bath, observing the *gaijin*—the foreigner—writhing in agony while they comfortably tolerated the heat, and then laughing as I quickly climbed out, my skin clean—but covered in second-degree burns. I couldn't wait.

Three days into the mission, I couldn't put off bathing any longer. Two upper-income Japanese college girls who had accompanied our team had also never bathed in public. Together, we dragged our feet to the bathhouse, paid our money, and followed the hallway fork to the left toward the women's side of the facility.

Soon wrapped modestly in towels, our clothes stuffed into lockers, we carefully entered what I call the pre-wash room like deer stepping into an open meadow. Around the large, fully-tiled room, spigots had been installed about knee-high. Small stools and little buckets sat near each faucet so that bathers could wash themselves completely before heading outdoors to soak in the 12 x 9 foot bath.

I washed and washed and washed myself, waiting for those two girls to lead the way to the ofuro outdoors and thus serve as distractions from my own entrance. But they were dawdling the same way I was. I wonder why I didn't just dry off, get dressed and leave; I was certainly clean. But at that time, for whatever reason, I felt compelled to complete the entire, proper bathing ritual.

Finally, I couldn't postpone the dreaded bath any longer. For days I had prayed that Jesus would deliver me from certain public humiliation; so far, He hadn't. I needed to get it over with, so I told the girls I was going in.

Wrapped in a towel, swiftly I walked outdoors over to the steps leading down into a bathing container that, to me, resembled a room-sized baptismal tank. Instead of a crowd, only two or three ancient Japanese women were there, soaking in water up to their necks. Their facial skin appeared dark and leathery and deeply lined, probably from working long days in the rice fields; *skin toughened enough to protect them from the hot water*, I thought to myself. I took a big breath, let the towel drop and quickly descended the steps, immersing up to my chin.

To my astonishment, the water temperature felt tepid! Moderately warm! Lukewarm, even. And very, very comfortable to my skin, like Michigan lake water in August. I exhaled the tension that had accumulated for weeks. My muscles relaxed as my body floated a little, and I playfully moved my arms around a few strokes, though this was probably not proper *ofuro* etiquette. All I could think of was that a whole village was not staring at me and the bath water was not burning my skin. All that worry for nothing.

My peaceful thoughts were suddenly interrupted by screams coming from behind me. I turned around to see my two student companions now in the water near the steps, faces in agony, bodies bobbing up and down in what apparently, to them, felt like hot, boiling water. The two young women remained in the bath about 15 seconds, then escaped, rushing back inside.

My mind took a long moment to sort through its confusion before I could acknowledge what had happened: God, I believed, had done something out of the ordinary for me.

I don't know how He did it any more than Old Testament characters Shadrach, Meshach, and Abednego knew how they didn't burn up when a wicked king threw them into a fire or how, afterward, their clothes didn't even smell like smoke. But those men were taking a public stand for God. Why would God go out of His way supernaturally for a fearful young woman who simply wanted to avoid personal embarrassment? And are deliverances always done in unexpected ways? Must we always enter the fire (or hot water) first?

Letting go of my questions, I began to focus my eyes on the peaceful garden that surrounded the bath like the setting for a jewel. I eased the back of my neck down onto the tiled, curved edge of the *ofuro*, allowing my near-weightless limbs to rest, suspended in the liquid mercy.

—Diane G. H. Kilmer, Tennessee

MULTI-PURPOSE MIRACLE

When I made Jesus my best Friend, I gained a sense of peace, purpose and inner joy that I had never known before. I wanted to tell everyone about Him, so they, too, could experience this peace and happiness. Unfortunately, as a child I experienced some rejection in grade school. As the years rolled on, I found myself striving to gain everyone's approval. Often, my silent fears of rejection caused me to clam up instead of sharing my faith with others. I knew the Lord still loved me, but I could not help but feel disheartened and guilty about this aspect of my life.

In the Bible scripture Philippians 4:6 we are told to not have anxiety about anything, but instead, tell God about the things that concern us. So, I began to pray, asking the Lord to please help me get over my fear of rejection.

Not long after I began bringing this request before God daily, my bus-driving job transporting special needs children and adults turned into a real pain in the butt—literally. A visit to the emergency room revealed I had a perianal cyst. After being referred to a surgeon, an outpatient surgery was scheduled.

By this time in my life, I had experienced four astounding physical healings from the Lord. To be honest, I totally expected God to heal me and never thought I would have to go through the surgery. Much to my surprise and bewilderment, the surgery date arrived, and I still had my perianal cyst. Surgery was performed, and I couldn't help but ask God, *Why didn't You heal me?*

For the following five weeks, I had to go as an outpatient to the surgeon's office, usually three times a week. The recovery process requires that the cyst cavity be packed with sterilized gauze, which needs to be changed daily (very painful, I might add). One of my daughters would come over and change the gauze on the days between office visits—which was very humbling to me.

Overall, the whole situation seemed like an inconvenience. I could not make sense of why God was allowing this to happen. Nevertheless, I was getting to know the surgeon and her nurses on a more personal level, and God always gave me the grace to keep a smile on my face.

The time came when the cyst cavity was healed, and the surgeon told me I did not need to come back any more. She then asked if I had any questions.

I was curious about something, so I asked, "I thought once the cyst cavity was healed, my *stools* would look normal again." She wanted to know what I was talking about. So I explained that for the past four years or so, my stools looked like thin little strings or ribbons, sometimes accompanied with blood. The doctor informed me the perianal cyst had nothing to do with these symptoms and told me I needed to have a colonoscopy.

The colonoscopy revealed two ulcerated masses and a fissure (a tear) in my bowels.

The surgeon told me that the portion of my bowels containing the masses needed to be removed and the fissure needed to be repaired. A surgery date was set for a couple weeks away. I was advised to take six weeks off from work for recovery.

The day before my scheduled surgery, I had a pre-op appointment. I wanted God to heal me, and so that morning I said a simple prayer.

In years past, I had received healings in various ways. Sometimes, I requested prayer at church. Other times, while by myself, I asked God to heal me. On some occasions I was healed instantly. Other times I stood in faith for weeks, even months, speaking God's Word over my malady, declaring such verses as "...by His stripes I am healed..." (Isaiah 53:5).

My most precious memory of being healed happened when I was a fairly new follower of Christ. I was in my early 20s and had been diagnosed with cancer in my face. At the time, I knew little to nothing about quoting "healing verses" from the Bible. All I knew was that I loved Jesus with all my heart, and He had forgiven me for a multitude of sins. The night before the scheduled cancer surgery, I simply said, "Jesus, if you wanted to heal me, You could." Jesuss urrounded me with His presence and gloriously healed me right then and there!

The day before my scheduled bowel surgery, I found myself saying the exact prayer I had said decades before: "Jesus, if you wanted to heal me, You could." Repeating these same words brought back the beautiful memory of that healing and reminded me of how truly great God's love and mercy is towards us.

This time after praying, I felt nothing happen whatsoever, but a few hours later when nature called, *everything* was back to normal for the first time in years!

That afternoon when I went to my pre-op appointment, the surgeon asked me if anything had changed. I had to tell her "yes." Of course, she wanted to know what had changed.

Responding honestly, I told her, "This morning I prayed and said to Jesus, 'If You wanted to heal me, You could'—then, a few hours later when I used the bathroom, my *stool* appeared completely normal for the first time in over four years." Looking very surprised, the doctor said, "I think we need to do another colonoscopy."

A second colonoscopy was performed, revealing only healthy bowel tissue. The ulcerated masses were gone and the fissure was healed! The surgeon and two nurses who had tended to my perianal cyst for the last several weeks stood in the room looking baffled as we all viewed my before-and-after films. A miracle had undeniably taken place for us all to see!

While we all stood in the examination room, I said, "This isn't the first time this has happened to me." Then I told them in detail about the time Jesus healed the cancer in my face.

The surgeon and nurses stood there listening intently, not making a peep. When I finished talking, the doctor came closer to me and said, "Let me touch you!" She then said the surgery needed to be canceled—there was nothing to fix!

Once back home I called my boss and told her about my miracle and that I would be able to drive my bus run after all.

The following workday everyone was surprised to see me. I had told all the parents and caregivers of the passengers I transported, as well as my fellow bus drivers and several teachers, that I would be gone for the next six weeks due to my upcoming surgery.

Now they were all asking, "What are you doing here?"

They peppered me with so many questions that I had no alternative but to tell them about my healing. To my great surprise, everyone was intensely interested and truly astonished when I told about the prayer I had said the morning of my pre-op appointment. Inspired by their favorable response, I told them some of my other past healings. One parent, who I particularly feared rejection from, asked me if I would pray for her. I was shocked! All my fears of rejection had been for nothing. I learned a great deal that day—especially that I had needlessly been letting fear keep me from sharing my faith with others.

That experience also taught me that it is important to trust God in all circumstances. There have been occasions in the past when I prayed in faith for a physical healing, but my symptoms remained. Such was the case when I asked the Lord to heal my perianal cyst. What appeared to me as unanswered prayer was, in reality, God orchestrating a much greater agenda.

Not only was He answering my prayers about getting over my fears of rejection, God let me experience the pleasure of telling others about His reality. I was greatly encouraged by the realization that the One who began a good work in me would be faithful to complete it until the day of Jesus Christ! (Philippians 1:6)

"And we know that in all things God works for the good of those who love Him, who have been called according to His purpose."

- Romans 8:28

—Nina Stellwagen, Michigan

IN GOD'S HANDS

My husband Mark started a septic service company in 2007. Due to a new county ordinance implemented soon after, thousands of residents were required to have their septic tanks pumped and inspected. We were suddenly swamped with work, and our phone was ringing off the hook!

I was a mother of four, trying to take care of the children and run the office end of the business from our home. Every day was hectic with little time to spare. A great deal of my time was spent on the phone writing down job information, answering customer questions or dispatching information to the crew. I was also doing all the bookkeeping. As a consequence, I was unable to spend as much time with the kids as I wanted to, and they often had to entertain themselves. Usually they were doing harmless things and making messes as kids often do.

At the time, my three-year-old son Joseph was going through a stage where numerous times each day he would pick up a little toy or two—often army men or small cars—and hide them under his shirt. Then he would come to me with a little, mischievous smile on his face, with his hand underneath his shirt, and say, "Mommy," letting me know he was hiding something from me. I would usually respond playfully: "Joseph, what do you have?" Often times he would quickly pull out his toy and laugh. Other times he would just give me that cute grin and then scurry away. For some reason he thought this was very funny. Joseph pulled this innocent little trick so frequently that I never gave it a second thought.

One day as I was sitting at the dining table doing paperwork, Joseph walked up to me with his hand under his shirt, smiling as usual. My mind was so preoccupied with the task at hand, that I only responded with a quick smile. At that moment, it dawned on me that I needed to switch a load of laundry from the washer to dryer. I got up from the table and headed toward the laundry room, while Joseph headed down the hallway toward his bedroom.

Suddenly I was stopped dead in my tracks with an urgency to see what Joseph had hiding under his shirt. Since this made little sense, I tried to dismiss the urge and started to take another step. Immediately the overwhelming sense of urgency flooded through me again. It was as though someone had suddenly stopped me and was pulling me to come along with them.

Without wasting another moment, I hurried to my son and reached under his shirt. Instead of the usual little toy, I was horrified to find a serrated steak knife! Instantly, my heart began to beat double-time. Joseph is an active boy, often climbing, jumping and running. In a flash I saw what could have happened, but did not. Then it hit me—God Himself had stopped a serious accident from happening! Filled with gratitude, I cried, "Thank You, Lord!"

As a believer in Christ Jesus, one of my biggest, daily, heartfelt prayers is a request for divine protection over my children. Every day I ask the Lord to teach my children to obey Him, and I request that He please keep them safe in His arms. Then I always thank Him. At that moment I knew those prayers were heard and that my precious little boy was not only spared from possible death or serious injury—he was in God's hands!

—Leah Gibson, Florida

MEMORY LOSS GONE

About ten years ago, I began having some frightening experiences with my memory. On numerous occasions, I would be driving down the road and suddenly have no idea where I was or where I was going. This caused extreme panic and fear, especially when it happened in the country. During phone calls, there were times when, all at once, I could not remember who I was talking to or what we were talking about. I had to keep a cheat list hidden to recall the names of the women in a small Bible study group I had been attending for years. Often times I could not remember my own grandkids names!

Daily indications like these spelled out clearly that my memory was seriously faltering. I did not want to tell anyone about this, including my husband. Hoping and praying no one would notice, I kept the problem to myself and tried to hide it as best I could. For two years, my memory loss only worsened. The reality was—I appeared to have the beginning symptoms of Alzheimer's.

At work, I began to feel guilt and pressure about my deteriorating memory. Memory loss in my type of job could pose serious risks for others. One day my "secret problem" nearly caused a tragedy at work. So, after nearly twenty years at the same job, I handed in my resignation. Everyone was told that I was pursuing new interests. The fear caused by my worsening memory was now stealing my freedom and robbing my joy.

One day I was watching Joyce Meyer's program *Enjoying Everyday Life* on TV. Joyce's teaching on victorious Christian living has always been an inspiration to me. But, on this particular broadcast, she made a statement that really caught my attention. She said something to the effect of: "One time the devil tried to get me to think I was getting Alzheimer's, and I thought to myself, 'I have the mind of Christ (1 Corinthians 2:16) and He doesn't have Alzheimer's! Not only that, God has given me a sound mind!' I commanded the devil in Jesus' name to take his hands off my mind, and started claiming and professing what the Word of God said about my mind!"

Joyce's words hit home and penetrated my heart! The thought popped into my mind, *Wouldn't the enemy have liked to silence Joyce Meyer? Her God-given teaching gift has had an impact on millions of people.* Another thought entered my mind, *Wouldn't the enemy like to keep me from doing God's plan for my life? According to Ephesians 2:10: I am God's workmanship created in Christ Jesus, with works prepared in advance for me to do!*

Inspired by Joyce's words, I decided to fight back. Following her example, I began proclaiming: "I have the mind of Christ and there is no way He has Alzheimer's! I have been given a sound mind—God's Word declares it! In the authority of the name of Jesus, I command you satan, get your hands off my mind! I claim a sound mind and a keen memory in Jesus name!"

Day after day, I kept professing God's Word over my mind with exuberance—even when I continued to experience symptoms of memory loss. My memory began improving daily. By the end of a few months, all my symptoms of memory loss were gone!

Now, no matter where I go, I can easily recall the names of any acquaintances. Episodes of suddenly not knowing where I am or where I am going no longer happen, nor is there any trace of fear that these will ever happen again. My mind seems to be keener than ever.

For over four years now, I have been back working with people. What I do now requires far greater focus and mental skills than my old job, and I am enjoying it immensely! In addition, I have been doing some public speaking and have even hosted a few seminars on various topics. I am full of anticipation about what is ahead for me as I seek God's will and plan for my life. God is truly wonderful and His Word is powerful!

"For God has not given us a spirit of fear, but of power and of love and of a sound mind."

- 2 Timothy 1:7 NKJV

—Anonymous

TURN AND RUN

In the mid 1940s, something happened to me that I will never forget. I was just eight years old at the time.

My dad had died the year before, leaving my mom to provide for me and my two brothers, Merle and Alan. Our family struggled financially, so in order to make ends meet, Mom planted a huge pickle (that is, cucumber) patch.

A couple times a week, Mom, Merle and I would get up at the crack of dawn and pick the pickles for three or four hours while Alan played nearby, where Mom could keep an eye on him. The pickles were put into gunnysacks, and then loaded into the car to sell to the pickle station, where they were put into salt brine and delivered to restaurants and stores. After that, we often bought groceries.

On one of our trips to town, we noticed the fair was going on. Of course, we kids wanted to go to the fair, so Mom decided to let Merle and me go while she bought some groceries. Since we had just dropped a load of pickles off and collected the money for them, Mom gave Merle and me each some money for all our hard work. Then she dropped us off at the entrance to the fair, told us to stay together and exactly what time she would be back to pick us up.

Merle was older than I was and wanted to go on a ride called the "Shoes." I was scared to go on it, so he told me, "You stay right here, because I'm going on it."

While Merle was getting on the ride, a man came and stood beside me and said, "How are you, young lady?"

My mom had always taught me to be polite to people, so I told him I was doing fine.

Then the man said to me, "Do you like candy?"

Happily, I said, "Oh yeah, I like candy!"

He said, "You know, my pickup is on the other side of the woods here, and I've got a whole big sack of candy, and I don't know what I'm going to do with all of it! You're welcome to have it, if you want to come with me and go get it."

A bag of candy sounded great, so I said, "Sure!" So, while Merle was on the ride, I headed out with this man to the north end of the big track that went around the fairgrounds.

When we arrived at the edge of the woods, the man said, "You've gotta come back in here with me. My truck is on the other side of the woods." So I followed him on a path that headed into the woods.

Soon we came to a narrow creek that was only about a foot and a half wide. Just on the other side of the creek was a nice, grassy area near a big tree. The man jumped across the creek and then sat down on the grass.

That brought me to a stop. I thought, Why is he sitting down when we're supposed to be going to get candy?

Then he said to me, "Come on and hop over here, and we'll go on to where my pickup is."

Just as I was about to jump across the little creek, I heard a voice over my right shoulder clearly and firmly say, "Sandra, turn and run!" Turning my head to the right, I looked to see who was talking to me. There was no one there! Quickly, I turned my head back facing the man and saw that he was starting to get back up.

Just then, I heard the voice again: "Sandra, turn and run!" This time the voice was almost shouting at me. That really scared me, and I took off running. I was going so fast that my heels were hitting my backside!

Following the path back through the woods, then on to the track around the fairgrounds, I finally got back to where the ride was. Merle had been searching all over for me and was extremely upset with me. I begged Merle, "Please don't tell Mama. She'll never let me go again."

Not wanting Merle to know what really happened, I told him I was just checking something out a little ways from where he was. For many years, I never told anyone about what happened that day. I am so grateful that God rescued me. There is not a doubt in my mind that the audible voice I heard that day telling me to "turn and run" was that of my guardian angel!

—Sandra Wedge, Michigan

THE SMALL THINGS

There was a time in my life when I trusted no one and depended solely on myself. My entire life's experience had been based on distrust, and I built high walls around myself for protection. At the age of seven, I asked Jesus into my heart, even though at the time I did not completely understand what I was praying. I simply knew there was a God and that I needed Him.

Because I grew up believing no one was trustworthy, I would not ask God to help me whenever I was in need. Then my nearly 16-year marriage ended just two months before our son was born. I was devastated. This life-altering trial caused me to cry out to God. The lack of money to meet every day needs became a serious issue.

One day my car had no more gas, and I had no money to put any into it. I needed to get back and forth to work every day. Not knowing what to do, I finally prayed, "Lord, I have no money, but I am learning that you will provide all that I need. Please help me. I need to drive this car without any gas in it. Can you do that for me?" For an entire week, I drove the car around without any gas in it!

That same week I needed to mow my lawn, but there was only a small amount of gas in the mower tank. Having mowed the lawn numerous times, I knew there was not enough gas to do the whole yard, which always took about an hour.

Again, I prayed and asked God to help me. After I mowed my entire lawn, I got off the mower and checked the gage, which read "empty." I took the lid off the tank to see for myself what I already knew must be true: The tank was bone dry! Again, God came to my rescue, and my trust and confidence that He would take care of me kept growing.

God began to work on many issues in my life through these small miracles He was doing for me. As summer became winter and my emotions were still on a roller coaster, God continued to teach me to rely on Him instead of myself during this difficult time in my life.

One day as I was folding laundry, I began to pray, telling God that I needed $5 to buy a gallon of milk and some bread. As I pulled some clothes out of the dryer, a dollar fell on the floor. Picking it up, I said, "Cool! Now all I need is four more!" As I continued to fold laundry, another dollar fell out on the floor! Soon another dollar tumbled out! By this time I was getting really excited, but was afraid to look through the laundry to see if the remaining $2 was there, so I just kept folding clothes. As you probably guessed, by the time I was done folding that batch of laundry, I had exactly $5!

God has done some big miracles in my life, and they were life changing, but I will always remember these small miracles as very precious. They were the beginning of my recognizing just how much God loves me—that He not only cares about the big things in my life, but also the small. Someday, I look forward to telling these cherished stories to my grandchildren!

"Trust in the Lord with all your heart and lean not on your own understanding; in all your ways acknowledge Him and He will direct your paths."

- Proverbs 3:5-6

—Tammy Barber, Michigan

SWOLLEN HEAD

Sometimes God works in mysterious ways, and we are not quite sure what He is up to—but I always feel sure that God is working out a good master plan. Such was the case many years ago when, for no apparent reason, my forehead and entire skull area began to swell. Although the depth of the swelling was only about one fourth inch thick, it was very noticeable. To the touch, the entire affected area had the consistency of a water-soaked sponge. When I pressed my fingers into the swollen area, deep indentations were left that remained for at least fifteen minutes. Knowing this was abnormal, I called the doctor's office and told them my symptoms. They told me to come in as soon as possible.

Directly after I arrived at the clinic, the staff took me to one of the patient rooms. Immediately, the doctor came in and began examining my head. I could sense he was alarmed.

After completing the examination and checking my vital signs, the doctor said, "This is not good." He proceeded to tell me two possible scenarios, both of them very serious. The doctor wanted me to go directly to the hospital. He was very disturbed when I told him I planned to attend our Thursday mid-week church service that evening and would ask for prayer concerning my symptoms. However, I agreed to check in at the hospital early the following morning, but informed the doctor there was a good possibility that I would no longer have any symptoms. The doctor did not share my enthusiasm or beliefs. Because I had personally experienced healings in the past, my faith was big.

That evening when I attended church, I requested prayer for my swollen head. God answered, and all the swelling quickly went away.

The following morning I went to the hospital, feeling sure God would want me to keep my appointment. When the doctor saw me and rechecked my vital signs, he was shocked. Everything was back to normal! Several times he said, "This is impossible! You've had a miracle!"

I learned that a short time later, someone invited the doctor to church. After attending several services, he commited his life to Christ.

I would not be surprised one bit if the only reason this incident happened, was so the doctor could see a demonstration of God's reality!

"When He heard this, Jesus said, 'This sickness will not end in death. No, it is for God's glory so that God's Son may be glorified through it.'"

- John 11:4

—Nina Stellwagen, Michigan

IT'S NEVER TOO LATE

Lou was in his late 80s and had just been brought home from the hospital by ambulance. He had been in a coma for the past three weeks, and the physicians could do nothing more for him. Now that he had been given only a few days to live, his wife Scottie wanted Lou to be able to die at home.

For five years I had been cleaning Scottie and Lou's house three days a week. During that time I learned that Scottie and Lou had both been previously widowed and that they had been married to each other for more than 35 years. Scottie confided in me that Lou had been a heavy drinker for most their marriage.

One day while I was cleaning their house, an incident happened that revealed some of Scottie's personal beliefs. She told me Lou had received a letter from one of his grandchildren that said they were praying for him to be born again. Scottie wanted to know what "born again" meant.

Happily, I explained to her how Jesus had died on the cross to pay the price for our sins and that anyone who invited Him into their

129

heart and life would be forgiven of all their sins and would be granted everlasting life in God's Kingdom.

Sounding disgusted, Scottie said, "That's what 'born again' means?!" Upon that remark she marched into their bedroom and removed a plaque from the wall that had the Bible verse John 3:16 written on it; *For God so loved the world that he gave his one and only Son, that whoever believes in him shall not perish but have eternal life.* Someone had given them the plaque, and Scottie had not paid any attention to it before. Scottie shoved the plaque into my hand and said, "Here, you take this. I don't want it in here anymore!"

During those five years of cleaning their house, I barely got to know Lou. He sat out on their screened-in porch for hours every day and rarely talked.

Shortly after Lou had been brought home to die, Scottie asked me if I minded staying at the house with him while she made a quick trip to the drugstore. Since Lou had been unresponsive for the last three weeks, Scottie felt assured there was nothing I would have to do concerning him. Gladly, I told her that would be fine and a few minutes later she was on her way.

Scottie had been gone about ten minutes when I was startled to hear Lou call out her name in a desperate-sounding voice! Rushing into the bedroom where he was, I said, "Scottie's not here. Can I help you?"

Sounding frightened, he cried out, "I'm dying! I'm dying!"

Silently I breathed a quick prayer asking the Lord to please help me know what to do and say. Seemingly, without thought on my part, these words just flew out my mouth: "Are you ready!?"

Lou immediately answered, "NO! Not quite!"

Still shocked that Lou was conscious and talking, I asked him what he meant by "Not quite."

He responded, "It's too late for me!"

I told him, "It's never too late!"

In a sorrowful whisper, he went on, "You don't understand. When I was eight years old, I asked Jesus to come into my heart at Sunday school. But I wandered away from Him and have lived a terrible life. Now it's too late for me!"

Again, I reassured Lou that it was not too late. Then I told him the story about the thief who hung on his own cross beside Jesus. He, too, was ashamed of how he had lived his life, yet he called out to Jesus in his final hours of life, saying, "Jesus, remember me when you come into your kingdom." Jesus answered him, "I tell you the truth, today you will be with me in paradise." (Luke 23:42-43)

After a couple more minutes of conversation, Lou became convinced that the Lord still wanted him. He began to sob, telling the Lord several times, "I'm so sorry. I'm so sorry." Then, with tears still streaming down his cheeks, Lou repeated a prayer after me, asking Jesus to forgive him and to come into his heart.

Wanting to be absolutely sure Lou understood what was going on, I asked him if he knew what had just happened. He smiled at me and in a weak voice said, "I just asked Jesus into my heart." Then Lou slipped peacefully back into his unresponsive condition.

Soon after, Scottie returned home. Joyfully, I told her what had transpired while she was gone. She did not share my joy. In fact, Scottie was very upset with me. At first it bothered me that she was so unhappy with me, but not for long. I realized that God had allowed me to be a part of a wonderful, divine appointment.

The more I thought about it, the more incredible I realized it all was. Lou had been unresponsive for the last three weeks, except for one, ten-minute window of time, while I was alone with him! As far as I know, Lou never spoke another word to anyone after his prayer. Soon after that day, he peacefully entered eternity, where he was lovingly welcomed by his Savior.

131

"What do you think? If a man owns a hundred sheep, and one of them wanders away, will he not leave the ninety-nine on the hills and go to look for the one that wandered off? And if he finds it, I tell you the truth, he is happier about that one sheep than about the ninety-nine that did not wander off. In the same way your Father in heaven is not willing that any of these little ones should be lost."

- *Matthew 18:12-14*

—Dolly Straley, Florida

NOTE FROM THE EDITOR: In the years that followed Lou's death, Dolly and her husband Bob continued to visit Scottie. Near the end of Scotties's life, after she had moved to an assisted living facility, she would allow Bob and Dolly to pray with her after their visits.

UPSIDE DOWN TRUCK

In 1970, when my husband and I purchased a blue Ford pickup truck, it seemed like everybody in the county had a blue Ford pickup! To make our new truck easy to recognize at a glance, we painted an orange stripe down each side of the truck, from the headlights to the taillights.

A few days later, my husband and I were heading to Marlette, Michigan, where we both worked at a motor home manufacturing facility. My husband was driving the company pickup, and I was following behind, driving our truck with the newly-painted orange stripe. We were hightailing it down Marlette Road doing 70 miles per hour. We should not have been driving that fast, but it was early in the morning, and there was not any other traffic around.

Suddenly, a vision appeared just outside my front windshield: I saw the truck I was driving, upside down with the wheels still spinning—the orange stripe clearly visible! I felt as if I were watching this frightening scene on a gigantic TV screen, life-sized and in full color! Terrified, I took my foot off the accelerator, feeling an urgency to get off the road. Slowing down, I eased off the road about 20 feet before the bridge. A steep embankment left very little room to pull over, but I scooted the truck off the road as far as I could. Finally stopped, I sat there shaking and bawling my head off. I was a complete, emotional mess.

My husband had already driven over the bridge, but soon realized I was no longer behind him. He turned around and came back to where I was parked. Hopping out of his truck, he came over and asked me, "What's the matter?"

Sobbing, I said, "I don't know. But I can't drive this thing anymore!"

He looked as if I might be losing my mind. But he went around to the back of the truck and looked under it. He came back and said, "I don't see anything wrong." Then he walked around the front of the truck and bent down to look under it. When he stood up, he looked as white as a ghost. Both of my tie rods were off!

The bridge just ahead of us was all torn up and in dire need of repair. After I calmed down some, my husband and I walked out on the bridge to inspect it. There were numerous, deep potholes; one of them went all the way down to the metal frame. Losing control of my vehicle on the bridge could have ended in tragedy!

God had to do something quite spectacular to get me to slow down and stop the truck before crossing that bridge. Seeing a vision of our truck upside down, brought me to a quick halt! I have always felt God's miraculous intervention spared me from a terrible accident that day—maybe even saved my life.

My near-accident has caused me to want to reach out and help others—not as an obligation, but simply out of a grateful heart for the love God has shown me. It is a comfort to know that He is in the ultimate driver's seat of my life!

—Sandra Wedge, Michigan

THE FINAL BLOW

I grew up in a Christian home. My parents took us kids to church every Sunday morning and evening, plus a midweek service. They saw to it that we attended all the youth group activities, as well as a Christian youth camp in the summer. My mom and dad lived exemplary Christian lives and did their best to instill godly values in us kids. Yet, in high school, I got in with the wild crowd and started drinking, partying, doing drugs and getting into trouble at school and elsewhere. At the time, there was no stopping me. I was bent on living life my way!

Shortly after high school graduation, I was in a serious motorcycle accident. A car hit me with such impact, eye witnesses reported seeing me fly up and over the power lines before crashing on the pavement below! After several months of recovery time and feeling that God had spared my life, I was fired up to change and live for God. But once I got back on my feet, I was soon back to my old ways. Drinking, partying and drugs took priority in my life during the next several years.

A few years after the accident, I got a job working in a rock quarry. For twelve hours a day, I drove a huge vehicle we referred to as a "YUK." At the quarry, areas of ground were blasted with dynamite, and then chunks of rock, dirt and sand were hauled to the processing plant less than a mile away.

The YUK could haul 30 tons of materials per load. Its tires were more than six feet high. The main body was made of steel, making any contact with electrical wires a potentially deadly hazard. For safety, the driver's cab was made completely out of fiberglass. Additional safety precautions were also implemented inside the cab: the steering wheel, gas and brake pedal were all covered in hard rubber, so they would not become electricity conductors.

Some of the trucks were getting old and were no longer up to code. Such was the condition of the YUK I was driving on what became a very memorable day. The rubber coating that was supposed to cover the gas and brake pedal was completely worn off, exposing the bare metal. The adjustment lever for the seat was not working either. Unable to move the seat forward, I put a block of wood on the brake and gas pedal for better access.

One day, while crossing over some railroad tracks at the quarry, an eight-inch railroad spike got stuck in one of my tires. At the service area, I raised the truck bed so that the tire could be checked. Upon completion, I was given clearance to go back to the work area.

After pushing the lever to lower the truck bed, I proceeded to head back to the quarry to pick up another load of materials. Unknown to me, the truck bed had not gone back down. Because the fiberglass cab is enclosed in an outer steel casing, which completely obstructs the driver's view of the truck bed, we relied entirely on our instruments. My warning light did not come on, and so I assumed the bed had lowered completely.

Unaware of the impending danger, I came to the area of the plant where the power feeder lines were located. Normally, the huge vehicle would have passed under the power lines without any problem. But the raised truck bed snagged the power lines and began snapping the poles! The vehicles are so huge and powerful that I did not detect anything unusual going on. My focus was drawn ahead to a pickup truck that was speeding towards me with its lights flashing. My gaze at the flashing lights was suddenly interrupted by bolts of electricity jumping from side to side off the metal frames of my mirrors! I brought the YUK to a halt. After being assured it was safe, I climbed out. Behind me was a trail of snapped power lines, cutting off electricity to the entire plant.

My supervisor came running towards me. He kept repeating, "I thought you were dead!" As he had been driving towards me, he had seen electricity dripping off the YUK in every direction, like rain off a roof. Even the yellow paint was melting off the truck.

The entire body of the YUK had been a mass conductor of

electricity. If I had touched anything metal inside the cab, then I would have been killed instantly. The only thing that separated me from the bare, exposed pedal on the floor was the block of wood I had placed there!

God had spared my life a second time, and I knew it. This second close call with death temporarily shook me up, but before long, I put God on the back burner of my life again.

Three months later, at the same plant, I asked to be given a job where I could make more money. I was transferred to the dynamite crew.

On the first day at my new position, my fellow crew members thought hands-on experience would be my best teacher. However, there was a slight problem. All three of them could barely speak English. The crew began giving me instructions, intending to tell me that there were six holes in the ground, each 10 feet apart. I was to put two bags of blasting powder in each of the six holes.

Picking up only fragments of their conversation, all I understood were the words "six" and "two" and something about the holes being 10 feet apart. After they finished instructing me, the crew backed the van containing the explosives up to the blasting site. The crew stayed in the van, and I went right to work.

In the back of the van were 12 rolls of blasting powder, packaged in plastic bags about four inches in diameter by three feet long. The holes the crew had drilled were thirty feet deep each. From where I was standing, only two holes were visible. Simple math told me: 12 rolls, two holes. So I loaded two holes each with six bags each of the blasting powder. Once the job was done, I informed the crew. We all went to an area about 1,200 feet away, and the crew chief ignited the explosives.

None of us were prepared for what happened next. The explosion was so powerful it shook the whole area, and we were all blown backwards! Rocks of all sizes, some weighing more than 100 pounds, were blasted skyward, temporarily vanishing from sight before falling back to the earth. The explosion blew out all the windows at our plant and cracked windows over a mile away. A crater was left in the earth that was 65 feet deep by nearly 200 feet across!

The explosion jolted me into the sobering realization, that only by God's mercy and love—I was still alive. This was the third time He had spared me from death. The final blow at the quarry was the wake-up call I needed to put God on the front burner of my life! That was the best decision I ever made. Now, instead of fearing death, I look forward to entering into eternity someday!

—Dave Straley, Tennessee

HEAVENLY BACK SURGERY

While in my early 20s, I was in two car accidents. One time a man ran the red light and hit my vehicle broadside. The force of the collision threw me sideways and the top of my head slammed into the passenger-side door.

A year or so later, I was briefly stopped on a secondary highway to make a left turn, when a man crashed into the rear of my car going 45-55 miles per hour.

After each of these accidents, I was disoriented for several minutes and sustained significant whiplash to my neck.

Apparently my neck was not the only part of my body affected by these mishaps. In the years that followed, my back became a growing source of pain—sometimes excruciating. Going places that required standing in one spot for any length of time was often a challenge. On occasion, I came close to abandoning my cart of groceries, because the pain from waiting in line at the checkout was nearly unbearable. The searing pain in my back often radiated down into my hips and legs. Sometimes I could barely crawl out of bed in the morning. For more than 15 years I frequented chiropractors to ease my pain.

One Sunday morning a guest evangelist spoke at our church. At the end of his message, he felt led by the Lord to pray for people needing healing. The man began naming various ailments, inviting the afflicted to come forward. Then, much to my joy, he said something like, "The Lord is going to heal backs." Immediately, I heard an inner Voice resound in my head: "That's you. Go!"

I quickly headed to the front of the church where a line was already forming.

When it was my turn to be prayed for, I began having the exact sensation I have had when being administered anesthesia just before surgery. I remember saying to the evangelist, "You better hurry, because I can't keep conscious much longer."

After saying those words, I fell unconscious to the floor and lay there for at least 30 minutes. I have no memory of falling to the floor nor did I hear or feel anything while lying there (although my husband later told me I was smiling).

When I had gone up front for prayer, the church was full of people. When I regained consciousness, nearly everyone was gone. My husband Eric sat in a folding chair, leaning over, staring at me with a big smile on his face.

When I got up from the floor, my back was 100% healed!

Nearly 20 years have gone by since that day, and my back has remained pain-free—except for two days a couple years ago when something very interesting happened. My episode began on a Friday morning:

I had bent over to pick up a 40-pound bag of wood pellets, when I wrenched my back. Instantly, I was in pain. Oddly, that same morning (after several years of experiencing good health), I awakened with a sore throat, fever, stiff neck, and coughing up yellow and green phlegm mixed with blood. I could barely function! I spent the rest of the day and evening in my recliner, taking fever and pain-reducing medicine every few hours.

The following morning nothing had changed, and my back was still in pain. I dreaded the afternoon coming; my husband Eric and I were scheduled to clean the church building. We had already traded with others to clean that day, so there seemed to be no way to get out of our cleaning commitment. With my head and back in such misery, I could not imagine how I was going to mop floors, clean toilets or do anything else.

My mind also started thinking of other activities I should cancel so that no one would be exposed to my illness. I decided not to attend church Sunday, nor visit my friend Nancy on Tuesday morning. But when I added the Tuesday night women's Bible study held at my house to my cancellation list, I remember thinking: *This is going to be embarrassing cancelling the Bible study, especially after the pep talk I gave the girls about healing last week!*

That is when the thought finally hit me: *What on earth am I doing accepting all these symptoms without so much as a small fight?!*

Scripture has taught me that it is important to fight the good fight of faith and not to dwell on doubts or entertain logic when seeking a healing. Instead, I needed to proclaim God's Word over my sickness and pain. Also, I have learned to seek The Healer in a far greater measure than the healing itself! If I am faithful to do these things—I can trust God with the ultimate outcome.

Isaiah 53:4-6 revealed to me that healing was an additional result or blessing of love and mercy that Jesus accomplished on the cross for us:

He took up our infirmities and carried our sorrows...He was pierced for our transgressions, He was crushed for our iniquities; the punishment that brought us peace was upon Him, and by His wounds we are healed...all of us have gone astray, each of us has turned to our own way; and the LORD has laid on Him the iniquity of us all!

These Bible verses made me realize that I could never earn or merit a healing; I simply needed to learn how to accept and receive this precious gift Jesus made available for us (Matthew 8:16-17).

As I began thinking of numerous healing verses and about how loving, merciful and forgiving the Lord is, another powerful thought occurred to me: the Lord would in NO way have anything to do with giving me back my bad back!

Right then and there, I began exuberantly proclaiming such prayers as, "Jesus, I receive what You did for me on the cross!"

"By Your wounds I am healed!"

"I receive all Your benefits—that You forgive all my sins and heal all my diseases!" (Psalm 103:2-3).

"I proclaim that the enemy's debilitating plans for me are cancelled in Jesus name! Instead, I receive health and healing in the powerful name of Jesus! I believe it—I receive it! Thank You, Lord!

I continued to thank and praise the Lord and declare every healing verse I could think of with exuberance, despite the symptoms I was experiencing. Numerous times when my physical symptoms would try to test my faith, I would remind myself that everyone mentioned in the Bible that Jesus healed—the blind, diseased, crippled, etc.—started out with something wrong! Then, I would simply say, "Of course I have symptoms. I wouldn't be believing for a healing if I didn't have symptoms!" If the enemy whispered in my ear that I didn't deserve to be healed, I would respond with: "Of course I don't, but Jesus died for my sins and was raised for my justification!" (Romans 4:8, 25)

For a few hours, I felt no change, but stood my ground proclaiming God's Word, also thanking and praising Him. By the mid-afternoon my back was feeling completely normal again, pain-free! My sore throat, cough, stiff neck and fever were gone! When my husband and I cleaned the church later that afternoon, there was not a single trace of evidence that anything had ever been wrong with me!

Thinking back about this episode, I have no doubt whatsoever that if I had not fought back, proclaiming God's Word over my situation, all my symptoms would have remained, and I would have undoubtedly cancelled numerous commitments.

"My son, pay attention to what I say; listen closely to My words. Do not let them out of your sight, keep them within your heart; for they are life to those that find them and health to a man's whole body. Above all else, guard your heart, for it is the wellspring of life."

- Proverbs 4:20-23

—Nina Stellwagen, Michigan

GO BUY GROCERIES

Many years ago when I was a young man, I had something really cool happen, which convinced me God was watching over my family and me. At the time, I had two young children, and my wife was in need of a kidney transplant. We moved to Climax, Michigan, where my wife was put on a waiting list for the transplant.

Finances were very tight. In fact, our finances were so limited that, at one point, we did not have enough money to buy food. I prayed to God for help. Even though this might seem crazy and a little ironic, God told me to go to the store, buy some groceries and write a check! I knew there was not enough money in our bank account to buy food. Trusting that I had heard from God, my wife and I went to the store, got some groceries and then wrote out a check for them.

When my wife and I returned home, we found an envelope stuck to our front door. We opened it to find a letter inside from a small, local club called The Four Leaf Clover. After finding out about my wife's illness and that she was on a waiting list for a kidney transplant, the club had generously taken up a collection for us.

Even though today, many years later, I am unable to remember the exact amount, I do remember their check was for $37 and some odd cents—the identical amount, to the penny, that I had written out the check for at the grocery store! That day I truly knew God was taking care of my family and that He hears our prayers.

—Tim Shaw, Florida

NOTE FROM THE EDITOR: While gathering stories for this book, I often read some of them to the 5th and 6th grade Sunday school class at church. One Sunday morning I selected this story and began reading it to them. Nearing the end of the story, I had just finished reading where the couple discovered the envelope attached to their door, with a check enclosed for the identical amount they had just spent on groceries. But before I had time to read another word, a very exuberant boy leaped to his feet and enthusiastically blurted out, "They should have bought more groceries!"

WHEN GOD TOUCHED ME

When I was a little girl, I thought miracles were all used up. I didn't see any amazing things happen or hear of any extraordinary events. But since then I've learned a few things about miracles, because God touched my life in a way I will never forget.

In 1997, I began having headaches. They were what I would describe as flashing headaches. I experienced short-lived pain that started at the base of my neck, and then went up and out through my eyes. The pain did not linger, but I was always left with a stiff neck. After running various tests and finding nothing wrong, doctors attributed my headaches to stress and tension.

On Friday, July 30, 1999, I experienced another flashing headache. I remember calling out to my husband Dave—then there was nothing. Dave somehow managed to get me into the car, then headed for the hospital in Mt. Pleasant. While en route I regained consciousness, but was talking with unusual speech patterns, resembling baby talk.

At Central Michigan Community Hospital (CMCH), my diagnosis was a ruptured cerebral brain aneurysm. The doctors did not expect me to live through the night. But as the night progressed I clung on to life, and I believe it was God's touch that made that possible. Amazing as this was, God was not finished showing His love and mercy.

Because there was no neurologist at CMCH, I was transferred by ambulance to MidMichigan Medical Center in Midland. After many tests and an angiogram, it was also discovered that there was an arteriovenous mass (a mass of tangled blood vessels) located above my left temple. A constricted blood vessel in this mass was causing the aneurysm in my brain stem.

The neurologist concluded it would be best to attempt to surgically fix the ruptured aneurysm. This course of action posed a high risk of severe brain damage, but time was the enemy. For the neurologist to perform this surgery he would need his colleague to assist him, but his associate was away on vacation in Michigan's Upper Peninsula. My husband was upset—every hour that passed reduced my chances of survival.

The decision was quickly made to transfer me to Harper-Grace Hospital in Detroit. There, more tests and angiograms were done. To everyone's amazement the angiograms revealed that the aneurysm had stopped bleeding! According to the neurologists, this was highly unusual.

With this new turn of information, a far less risky procedure was now possible. Instead of performing an invasive surgery in the brain stem, a stent, going up through the groin, could be placed into the affected blood vessel to keep its walls from ballooning any further. Now it is clear why the surgeon's associate was away on vacation. God intervened again! But was He done demonstrating His power?

No, not yet.

Numerous friends, family members and prayer chains were notified, and many prayers were going up for the surgeons to successfully insert the stent. But, to Dave's devastation, the procedure failed. The blood vessel had a kink in it and the stent could not be properly placed. Now there was nothing to do but wait for the vessel to rupture again, or do the surgery in the brain stem that held a high risk for brain damage.

After waking up from the procedure, I will never forget the grim look on Dave's face when he said to me, "Betti, the stent didn't work." All I could say to him at the time was, "I'm ready," knowing in my heart that I was ready to meet God, should He decide to take me to my eternal home. But God had other plans for me.

Later that night the neuroradiologist came looking for my husband and found Dave in the hallway walking toward my hospital room. With exuberance in his voice, the neuroradiologist said, "Mr. Bergman, Mr. Bergman! Come and see!"

He took Dave to a room where all the pictures of my aneurysm were displayed. After studying the X-rays and blood flows, it was discovered that the blood was flowing in the opposite direction than originally determined in the kinked blood vessel. The placement of that stent would have caused the aneurysm to balloon even further. The added pressure would more than likely have caused a deadly rupture! How fortunate it was to have that little kink. And it was truly amazing that the correct direction of blood flow was revealed to the doctors. Was God's hand in these events? I really believe so. And He still was not finished with His work.

With this new insight about the direction of blood flow, the neurologists decided that another surgical approach was possible: to untangle the knot of blood vessels in the arteriovenous mass.

The big day arrived for the surgery. I was now in a room just outside the operating room. Dave had just left after giving me a kiss and squeezing my hand. I was all alone and knew how difficult and dangerous the surgery would be. I didn't know if I would wake up, or whether I'd be the same if I did. So I prayed. It was a simple prayer. There was no bargaining with God or begging for forgiveness. All I said was, "Whatever You want, Lord."

At that moment a wonderful peace washed over me. I have never experienced such peace. I'm sure it was the peace that Paul described in Philippians 4:6-7: "Do not be anxious about anything, but in everything, by prayer and petition, with thanksgiving, present your requests to God. And the peace of God, which transcends all understanding, will guard your hearts and your minds through Christ Jesus." And guard my heart and mind, He did!

After twelve and a half hours of surgery, the knot of blood vessels in the arteriovenous mass was successfully untangled, thereby collapsing the aneurysm by releasing the pressure to the affected blood vessel. And here I am to tell about it. I give all praise and glory to our loving Lord and Creator who guided that scalpel. I was truly blessed. But His loving touch extended well beyond me and my family.

During the time I was hospitalized in Detroit, Dave met a man named Darryl who had actually taken up residence in the ICU waiting room. Darryl's wife, Veda, had a mysterious bacterial infection and had been in a coma for three months. Dave reached out to Darryl by talking to him, bringing him meals, and trying to comfort him.

One day Darryl asked Dave, "Why are you being so nice to me when you have your own problems?"

Dave answered, "Because I know Jesus."

After a lot of prayer and discussions together, Darryl decided he wanted what Dave had. So with Dave leading the prayer, Darryl invited Jesus into his heart to be his Lord and Savior! God was there extending His saving grace and mercy.

After Darryl came to know Jesus, he asked Dave to pray for his wife Veda. The physicians had no hope for her recovery. With the doctor's permission, Dave went into Veda's room and placed his hands on her shoulder and prayed for her. He asked for God's mercy and healing, but also for His Will to be done. Five days later Veda came out of her coma! Her bacterial infection was gone, and Darryl was informed that she could go home after completing some necessary physical therapy. Now I understand it was no accident that I was sent to Harper-Grace Hospital—it was one of God's divine appointments! Is there any limit to God's power?

So what about that little girl who thought all miracles were used up? Well, she has learned valuable lessons from these experiences, including that what appear to be frightening setbacks and unanswered prayers can actually be God at work!

I have also learned that God is present and listens to the pleas of His people. He does things in His own way and in His perfect timing, even when it makes no sense to us. The Apostle Paul says in Romans 8:28: "And we know that in all things God works for the good of those who love Him, who have been called according to His purpose."

Isn't it amazing how Our Lord and Creator orchestrated all these events surrounding a bulge in a tiny blood vessel way down in a brain stem? He knows what is best for us, and His every touch sends waves of love, mercy and grace far and wide.

—Betti Bergman, Michigan

BIBLES TO CHINA

Specific locations and dates will not be given in my story because I was part of a team that smuggled Bibles into China. Bibles are not illegal in China. In fact, they print them, but their pages have been edited to suit the Chinese Communist Government. All the miracles have been removed, as well as the book of Revelation and most prophecies. Chinese individuals caught with an unauthorized Bible could face a prison sentence.

Thousands of Chinese people become Christians every day. The true believers and followers of Jesus must meet secretly in places known as "house" or "underground" churches. Very few of these believers have access to unedited Bibles, including the pastors. The mission of our team was to smuggle Chinese study Bibles specifically for the pastors and leaders of the house churches. One Bible in Chinese can be used to minister to hundreds of lives.

Our team smuggled approximately 1,300 Bibles, weighing a pound and a half each, past the Chinese border stations. Every day's plan of operations began with prayer. We also had family and friends in the United States praying for us. Observing God answering prayers and doing miracles was awesome!

Time and again, we witnessed backpacks and bags filled with Bibles pass through the X-ray machine undetected while border guards closely monitored the screens! This is especially remarkable, considering books are easily detected in X-ray.

A couple of instances caused us to assume that God must have a sense of humor. One of our team members had 60 Bibles in a large duffle bag, with a smaller bag strapped onto it containing 10 more Bibles—an unusually large number of Bibles to attempt to smuggle at one time. The total weight of his luggage was 105 pounds.

When the border guards noticed our team member having difficulty lifting his bags onto the baggage conveyer, they lifted them on for him. Then the Bibles passed through the X-ray machine without detection!

Another time, when an elderly woman on one of our teams approached the baggage check area, she passed out cold. We watched as five Chinese border guards loaded her into a wheelchair, and then pushed her through customs—carrying her bags of concealed Bibles for her!

One day as our team was taking Bibles into China's interior, we needed to board a train. As we approached the passenger check area, the guards discovered a screwdriver in a man's suitcase just ahead of us. The commotion caused by security wanting to know why the man had the screwdriver was so huge that our entire group walked right past the guards and boarded the train, unnoticed, without any of our baggage getting checked! God was truly watching over us.

One afternoon something happened to me that every team member dreads. My bags had just gone through X-ray. After picking them back up, I started walking away when a guard came up behind me and asked me to come back and show him what was in my bags.

My heart pounded as I watched him open my backpack. In broken English, he asked me, "Are these Bibles?"

Reluctantly, I told him, "Yes."

Then he started looking through the rest of my bag, observing all the other Bibles. He said, "Are these all the same?"

Again, I told him, "Yes."

He then closed my backpack, set it down and said, "Go ahead." This amazed me—that just does not happen! I glanced at my watch and noticed it was 3:25 p.m.

Later, I found out that my parents were praying for me during that very same hour. There is exactly a 12-hour difference in time, from my home state of Michigan and China. My parents were both lying awake in bed, unable to sleep.

At 2:30 a.m. their time, they felt led to pray for me. They prayed for 45 minutes, with requests to the Lord such as, "Please blind the border guards' eyes. Please let the Bibles get through the border checks and X-ray undetected. Please give the guards a change of heart. Please let these Bibles reach those with a hunger to know You." Their prayers ended mere minutes before the guard looked in my backpack!

One day our team was given the rare opportunity to meet in a hotel room with some of the Chinese pastors. After sharing some personal testimonies with each other, we asked them some questions.

Knowing these pastors risk severe repercussions for speaking about their faith to others, we asked, "How do you know when to talk to people about Jesus?"

For a minute, they appeared puzzled, as if they did not understand the question. We started to rephrase the question in a way we thought would make the translation clearer. They interrupted us, saying, "No, no. We understand. But why would we want to wait to tell others about Jesus?"

We asked the pastors what the consequences could be if they were caught evangelizing.

Cheerfully, they told us, "Things are so much better now. It used to be bad. They used to put us in prison for 10 years. Now it's only five!" The Chinese pastors enthusiastically desired to share their faith with others, despite the costly risks.

We told the pastors we would pray that things would not be so hard for them.

They told us not to do that, noting that persecution had caused their personal faith and their churches to grow. They preferred, instead, that we pray for those who are imprisoned and undergoing trials because of their faith.

The Chinese Christians live their lives much like the early

followers written about in the Bible's book Acts of the Apostles. They embrace the possibility of persecution, imprisonment or losingtheir life as a privilege to honor the Lord. The government's attempts to extinguish Christianity in China have merely fanned the flames of the Holy Spirit.

The opportunity to go to China to see what God is doing and to participate in it was an incredible experience. We can all learn from the Christians in China!

Joshua Prewett, Michigan

THE PORTHOLE

NOTE FROM THE EDITOR: The following story is so bizarre that I hesitated to put it in this book, but I know it is authentic because it happened to me. When this incident took place, there seemed to be no apparent reason for it, yet I know that nothing happens in the life of a child of God without a reason. The Bible says: "... all things work together for good for those who love God, who are called according to His purpose" (Romans 8:28, RSV).

For several years, I drove a bus for a company that transported special-needs children and adults. The children attended programs at various schools, while many of the adults went to Mid Michigan Industries (MMI), a facility that provided jobs and activities uniquely suited for these special individuals.

At the time of this incident, two of our company buses were transporting passengers to and from MMI in Alma. We dropped our clients off in the morning and picked them up again in the afternoon.

The MMI building had a large paved lot, with parking spaces arranged so that buses and other vehicles could drive full circle around the lot. In the afternoons, our company's buses were scheduled to arrive first. I always parked my bus at a precise spot—near the end of the front of the building and slightly to the left around the curve. The other bus driver would pull up to the left of me, but the rear of her bus would extend about five or six feet behind mine so that she had clear access to open her wheelchair lift on the rear, passenger side of her bus.

One day I arrived at MMI five minutes ahead of schedule and decided to go inside to use the restroom. The bathroom, located just inside the front door of the building and a few steps to the right, had no windows.

Within a minute after I entered the restroom, something astonishing happened. An area about a foot wide by perhaps eight inches high, resembling the porthole of a ship, just seemed to meltaway in the wall! The edges to this opening were hazy, but I could clearly see the entire parking lot as I peered out the porthole, which was at my perfect eye level.

Moments after this opening appeared, I watched as our other company bus pulled into the MMI entrance. The bus drove the full length of the lot and came to a stop, but was not parked in its usual proximity to mine. Then I clearly observed that the woman driving the bus was not the usual driver, but one of the substitute drivers from Mt. Pleasant. She got out of her seat and walked to the back of her bus. My view was crystal clear and in full color, as if I were watching these things on a TV screen!

Suddenly, the porthole vanished, and the wall looked completely normal again. Stunned, I remember thinking, *Did this really just happen?! I just saw through the wall! This can't have happened!* Although disbelief wanted to take over, the clear memory of this fantastic experience lingered in my mind!

Within seconds I raced out of the building to see if what I had just watched through the porthole had really happened. The other bus was parked exactly where I saw it through the porthole. The substitute driver from Mt. Pleasant was still in the back of her bus! (The usual driver had said nothing to me about being gone that afternoon.)

This incident was so unbelievable that I did not tell anyone at the time. Later, I told a few close friends and some family members.

For some reason God allowed me to see through a wall! Why? Only He knows. While I was collecting stories for this book, God brought this strange occurrence back to my thoughts with the keen sense it was to be included in this book directly following the story BIBLES TO CHINA. Apparently someone needs to know that, if necessary, God can enable them to see through a wall!

—Nina Stellwagen, Michigan

155

CAN YOU HEAR THE ANGELS SINGING?

Leita was one of my best friends while we were growing up. We went to the same small country church, youth group and school. Leita and her brother Roy, along with my brother Dan and I, used to sing as a quartet in church. At school, we were in choir where we often sang together in trios and quartets. Leita had a beautiful soprano voice.

After graduating from high school, Leita went out of state to Bethel College in Indiana. She returned to our hometown her sophomore year to attend Central Michigan University, where I was a freshman.

One day in early fall while we were walking up the stairs at the University Center, Leita fell and was unable to get up by herself. By the end of that week, she had a diagnosis of a very aggressive bone cancer. Leita had a strong faith in God and maintained a positive attitude. She was also very creative and thoughtful. When Mother's Day came, even though she was extremely weak, Leita insisted on going to church so she could personally hand out her own homemade corsages to all the mothers. That was just part of her beautiful personality.

By early June, Leita was in the hospital to stay. My dad and I both worked in the lab, where Dad was the laboratory supervisor. Both of us were gifted at drawing blood from patients whose veins were difficult to get. Leita had become one of these patients. Soon she was semi-conscious much of the time and often did not recognize familiar faces. At this point, those who loved me, thought it would be best if I did not draw her blood anymore. There was concern it might be too emotionally painful for me. Although watching Leita deteriorate was very difficult, I still had a desire to spend time with her.

On June 20, the lab received STAT orders for blood work on Leita. It was lunchtime, and I should have tried to locate my dad to do the job. But he was not in the lab when the order came in and

I had been longing to see my friend. This was my chance. I headed for Leita's room.

Entering the room, I found the family gathered around her bed. My practice has always been to talk to the patient while I am drawing their blood, whether they are conscious or not. This time was no different. Even though she appeared unresponsive, I said, "Leita, I have to draw some blood."

She opened her eyes and said, "Marie, you cut your hair." Needless to say, we were all shocked!

Leita and I began talking as if we had never missed a single day. She wanted to know all about my boyfriend (who is now my husband) and other things that were going on in my life. Somehow, I sensed that this time was very important.

After I finished drawing Leita's blood and was about to leave the room, she started talking again. She asked me if I could hear the singing.

Not being sure what she meant, I asked her, "What singing?"

She said, "Can't you hear the angels singing? It's so beautiful!"

As I returned to the lab, I felt overjoyed that Leita had recognized me and that we had enjoyed such a wonderful conversation! About forty minutes after leaving her room, my dad found me and wanted to know if I had a minute.

In my heart, I already knew what he was going to tell me, and I said, "She's gone, isn't she?"

He said, "Yes, she died about 20 minutes ago."

Later I found out that after I left Leita's room, she returned to an unresponsive state. Her last words to me and her family were about the angels singing! The expression on her face as she spoke those final words will be forever etched in my memory. She looked so peaceful and radiant, even though her body was thin and frail.

After all these years, I still feel thankful that God opened a door that allowed me to spend those final minutes with my friend. I am convinced it was a divine appointment. Only God knew that 20 minutes after our visit, Leita would be in His very presence and singing with the angels!

—Marie Root, Michigan

JUST IN TIME

I had just received the sad news that our dear family friend Lola was dying of cancer. The early signs had gone unnoticed. Now her body was ravaged with the disease.

My mind wandered to the time, not long before, when we were both living in southern Arizona. Lola was a close friend and neighbor of my husband's grandparents. To us she was like a bonus grandmother. When we visited them, she would usually drop in, offering each member of my family a tight hug and warm greeting.

Lola laughed easily. She listened to us with genuine interest. She was as proud of my husband's accomplishments as she would be her own grandson's. Lola would settle her 80-year-old frame on the floor and play with our children as if they were her own great-grandchildren. There was so much to like and admire in this spunky woman who embraced life and those around her.

We had already said our goodbyes a year before, when we moved to our home state of Michigan and she to Canada to be with her son and his family. Now she was hospitalized and suffering great physical pain, which troubled me. However, a significantly greater concern formed in my mind—the all-important question of where Lola would spend eternity.

I was struck with the awful realization that I did not know if Lola knew my Savior. It pained me to acknowledge that we had never once discussed Christ with her and the good news proclaimed in the Bible: "For God so loved the world, that he gave his only begotten Son, that whosoever believeth in him should not perish, but have everlasting life." (John 3:16, KJV)

Her time was running out. I felt a strong urgency to do something. Phone conversation was now too difficult for Lola. The 2,000 miles that separated us made a visit out of the question. So it came down to a letter.

My first attempts to write Lola seemed futile, which made me feel irritated with myself. How hard could it be to share God's love—the most important influence in my life—with someone special to me? In addition, worry consumed me—primarily fears of offending her, her family or my husband's.

That night I barely slept and felt literally ill over Lola. Although my children's needs occupied me the following morning, Lola was heavy on my heart. Later that day, when I told a friend about my dilemma, she boldly told me to "Just do it!"

Her words compelled me to face a blank computer screen once again. Frustrated with my obvious inability, I came to God, needy and completely dependent on His ability. This time writing the letter was different! The words flowed easily, and I sensed that what had been my letter to a friend became God's letter to His dear child. I hurried to the post office.

My doubts resurfaced those next days, but I did not have to wait long before my husband's grandma called to give us the news. Lola had died, but that was not the end of her story.

Lola's son said the letter arrived only a day or two before she passed away. He read the letter to her, and then Lola wanted to hear it re-read several times. At that point, she was so weak that talking was very difficult. However, bit by bit, Lola managed to lift a simple prayer to Heaven, asking Jesus to be Lord of her life.

Her son described the change that came over her after she prayed. Before the prayer, Lola's struggle had escalated to the point of her frantically pulling at her IVs. After receiving Christ as her Savior, she became calmer and appeared to have true "peace of mind." Furthermore, Lola expressed a desire for all her family members, particularly her grandchildren, to receive copies of the letter.

Few things have blessed me so much in my life as this incident! I tremble to think of how my God operates. The Bible tells us that God's power is made perfect in our weakness (2 Corinthians 12:9). I was simply the pen in His Hand to copy a letter of Love.

Often I have longed for another visit with Lola. But I know that when I go to Heaven, we will have one, joyous reunion. I can just imagine her smiling, laughing face, and the joy she must have being with God!

—Kris Ratkos, Michigan

THE STILL CENTER OF THE STORM

It was a dark and stormy night. We were newlyweds, my spouse and I, driving in the middle of the night "straight through" to Abilene, Texas, from Michigan after our honeymoon. All our worldly possessions were packed behind us in a small U-haul trailer attached to the used car my new in-laws had given us as a wedding present.

Now I strained to see the road ahead through a watery, blurred windshield, while my husband slept soundly in the passenger seat beside me. The dashboard clock said three a.m. The adrenaline rush that had come with the exhilaration of being on our own, headed to our first home, had all drained away. My eyelids were becoming too heavy to keep open—I needed to pull over and sleep.

But there had been no sign of civilization for hours; no parking lot or rest stop or any break in the relentlessly narrow, bare, no-shoulder, two-lane highway. Finally, my rain-dulled headlights revealed a wide shoulder of road just ahead, a slight rise with overgrown bushes that offered safety from this torrential flooding.

In the blinding rain, I parked on the rise, turned off the engine, and expected to fall right to sleep. But instead, in the darkness, I felt an urgent nagging inside me to back the car off of the rise—trailer and all.

Without thinking, I obeyed the urge, too exhausted to argue with such irrationality. I turned the key, reversed the gear, and rolled straight back a foot or two. Since I don't remember a thing after that, I probably fell asleep within seconds of shutting off the engine.

I don't know how long I'd been asleep, when suddenly a loud, thunderous BOOM! startled us awake. The continuous roar rolling only inches in front of our car materialized in the downpour into a passing train speeding along its track. I quickly realized that my first parking spot had been directly on a railroad track!

My obedience to the urgent feeling had saved us.

I didn't know it right then, but eventually, over time, I came to believe that those pressing, restless urges are one of the ways the Holy Spirit of Jesus communicates with me, sometimes even warning me of danger. Of course, I can't prove it and a few other possible explanations can be suggested—all equally unprovable.

But over the past four decades these nudges sometimes come from a Voice I can recognize who tells me the truth, comforts me, gives me direction, and reminds me of what I've already learned so that I can stay on the road toward spiritual safety and maturity. This unseen Helper behaves exactly as Jesus had promised to His worried disciples the night before He died. So I pay attention.

—Diane G. H. Kilmer, Tennessee

THE PHONE CALL

"Now this is the confidence that we have in Him, that if we ask anything according to His will, He hears us. And if we know that He hears us, whatever we ask, we know that we have the petitions that we have asked of Him." (1 John 5:14-15, NKJV)

My sister Betty was six years older than me and probably told by my parents to watch over me almost every day. She became my mentor and was really a second mother to me as we grew older. For several years, I even lived with Betty and her husband. She and I were very close.

When God took Betty "Home" at the young age of 45, I was devastated. She was a very giving person who was quick to share whatever she had, always thinking of those who were less fortunate. In the four months that Betty lived after a major blood clot took most of her upper intestine, she literally starved to death. Her weight at the time of her death was only 60 pounds. Her slow, agonizing death was horrifying to watch and seemed so inappropriate for a wonderful person like her.

Even though I had been raised in a Christian home, my faith was severely tested. It was hard for me to believe that God would allow such a thing to happen to someone like Betty, as well as to her family. Although I continued to pray, I was unsure if my prayers were being heard. The grief did not let up for several months, and I slacked off in my attendance at church.

Near the end of Betty's life, all the medications she was on and her deteriorating physical condition had taken its toll on her. She was not the same; the bubbly, happy Betty was gone. The dark side of human thought began to torment me. Thoughts about how Betty was, and where she had been whisked off to, plagued my mind. Was Betty really OK? Was she at peace now? Not knowing the answers to these questions consumed me.

Then one night I dreamed that I received a phone call. The voice on the other end of the line was a big, resonant voice. This booming, reassuring voice said, "I have someone who wants to talk to you!" Instantly I knew it was God's voice with the answer to my prayers.

The next voice I heard was clearly Betty's. She said, "You know where I am!" She sounded so bubbly! Although I cannot remember the exact words that were spoken in our "phone call," it left me feeling assured that Betty was experiencing wonderful peace and happiness. Our conversation did not seem to last very long. Suddenly my feet felt very cold as I awakened to find myself standing on the tile floor in our kitchen with the telephone at my ear!

I may never know the answers to some things in this life, but that night God responded to my prayers in a real and powerful way. From the moment I heard that resounding voice on the phone, I knew it was God, and that Betty was OK, living in the glories and bliss of heaven! To hear Betty's own voice assuring me of her happiness was an added blessing beyond words for me. Following that phone call, relief and peace came over me instantly. I was able to move on in life with a huge weight lifted off my shoulders. WOW! God is so good!

—Jean Allen, Michigan

DIVINE APPOINTMENT

One morning I was sitting in my favorite chair in the living room, having a cup of coffee and reading my Bible, when my grown daughter Leah entered my thoughts. She had been going through a trial, and some Bible scriptures popped into my mind that I thought might be helpful to her. I promptly jotted them down on a piece of paper.

Later that afternoon I went to the computer and began typing out a letter of encouragement to my daughter, which I planned to email to her as soon as I was finished. Just as my letter was nearly completed, the phone rang. The caller was Duane, an old friend of one of my sons.

Duane and my son used to hang around together during high school and got into their share of trouble! Now, many years later, Duane is a dedicated follower of Jesus, attending college in pursuit of a career in the Lord's service. Seldom have I known anyone who devotes as much time to Bible study and prayer as Duane does. When he calls from time to time, he usually ends the conversation by asking, "Is there anything you would like me to pray for?" Of course, I always say yes because Bible scripture says, "The prayer of a righteous man is powerful and effective." (James 5:16b)

To be honest, this time when Duane called, I was disheartened. Nothing against Duane, but I was on a roll writing my "inspirational" letter, and just wanted to finish it and get it e-mailed. I quickly breathed a silent prayer for a more Christ-like attitude.

Duane and I talked for a while, then as usual he asked if I would like prayer for anything. After thinking it over for a moment, I told him I would like prayer for my children. There was silence on the phone for a few seconds, then Duane said, "I really feel led to pray for your daughter Leah." *How peculiar,* I thought. *Here I was writing to her when he called.* I was surprised Duane even remembered her name; he had not seen Leah in at least fifteen years, and he certainly knew nothing of the struggle she was currently going through.

Duane began his prayer. Within a couple minutes, I was dumbfounded by what I was hearing. Duane was praying for Leah as if he had been given a detailed description of her problem. I remember thinking, *This is incredible. This has to be from God!* I felt even more excited when, near the end of Duane's prayer, God spoke to him and said my daughter would soon triumph over her trial. I could hardly wait to tell Leah about this word from God, confident it would encourage her.

The minute our call ended, I got right back on the computer to finish the letter. Briefly, I told my daughter about the phone call and how Duane felt led to pray for her. Next, I typed out Duane's entire prayer to the best of my recollection, knowing it would confirm to Leah that God inspired his words. To conclude the letter, I wrote in parentheses: "(I think it was a divine appointment!)." To my shock, without my touching any settings on Microsoft Works, the statement appeared on the computer screen as follows—in bold, font size 16 lettering!

(I think it was a divine appointment!)

Unbelievable! Type size does not change in the middle of a paragraph, nor does lettering change to bold print on its own! God was confirming to my daughter in an astonishing way that He was aware of her battle and she would one day have the victory. God is so good!

"O LORD, you have searched me and you know me. You know when I sit and when I rise; You perceive my thoughts from afar. You discern my going out and my lying down; You are familiar with all my ways."

- Psalm 139:1-3

—Anonymous, Michigan

AT HEAVEN'S GATE

NOTE FROM THE EDITOR: This story is about my mother, Dolly Straley. While we were growing up, Mom told us kids some memorable stories about her life. The following is one of my favorites and very meaningful to me.

In 1949, my mother, only 21 at the time, stayed at home to take care of my brother Dan, nearly three, and my sister Marie, who was a year and a half old. My brother Dave and I had not been born yet. My dad was the pastor of a small country church.

One day my mother became extremely ill. Her head began hurting, and she had severe pain in her stomach. Soon she began throwing up. Sensing that her illness was serious, she told my dad to take her to the hospital. At Central Michigan Community Hospital in Mt. Pleasant, Mom's gallbladder was removed. Her lungs, found to have a number of puss sacs on them, were scraped.

For the next several days, Mom continued to have frequent bouts of vomiting that the physicians were unable to control. Her health continued to deteriorate. By the end of a week and a half of being in the hospital, Mom had grown gravely ill. Mom's physician, Dr. Lionel Davis, ordered a 24-hour watch. A family friend, Maxine Bumgart, was one of the nurses who spent her shift stationed in Mom's room. During the night, Mom had an unforgettable dream:

She began to climb a tall flight of stairs. What appeared to be a long way off at the top of the stairway was a white gate. Mom knew if she could reach the gate, her troubles would be over, and she would get the help she needed to get better. Every step she took was labored, but her intense desire to reach the top of the staircase inspired her to continue.

When Mom had finally climbed the last step, she was completely exhausted—but what she saw next was startling. Just beyond the gate was a place so beautiful that it defied human experience.

Plush, green grass in a hue and intensity Mom had not seen before

Plush, green grass in a hue and intensity Mom had not seen before covered the ground as far as the eye could see. Never before had grass seemed so alive! Not a single blemish could be found in this extraordinary, almost carpet-like lawn.

In stunning contrast, gorgeous flowers in vibrant colors were masterfully placed in this heavenly landscape. The perfection and loveliness of each flower and the depth of color was breathtaking. Right near the gate were exquisite red roses. Overhead was a magnificent blue sky. Celestial light flooded this place. The atmosphere was pure joy!

Off in the distance, surrounded by a bed of yellow flowers, children were playing. Mom could hear their laughter and sense their delight. They were indescribably happy and having the most marvelous time. Everything within my Mother wanted to go join them.

Just then, Jesus came through the gate. He was wearing a long, gown-type white robe with a sash around His waist. My mother felt bathed in a compelling, powerful love. Instantly, she had a longing to remain near Jesus forever.

Mom expressed to Jesus how much she wanted to enter through the gate and stay with Him in that wonderful place. She was deeply saddened when He said, "It's not yet time. Your work is not finished, my child. You must go back."

My mother went on to explain to Jesus how weak and tired she was and that she had climbed all those stairs to reach the gate. She remembers saying to Jesus (to her amusement now), "You don't understand. I just had surgery, and I'm not supposed to climb stairs."

Jesus spoke to her again with great love and tenderness, saying, "The going down will be easier." There was an immense, but loving authority in His voice that brought the undisputable knowledge that she must return to her life on earth. Jesus then left and went back through the gate.

Heartbroken that she could not remain with Jesus, Mom began to climb down the stairs. After descending only a couple steps, she awoke from her dream.

Her arms and body were icy cold to the point of numbness, and she was having difficulty breathing. Mom remembers Nurse Bumgart scurrying off and returning with other nurses, who immediately began taking her vital signs.

The following two nights my mother had the identical dream! Each time, Jesus walked through the gate, encompassed her in a great wave of boundless love, but then would tell my mother her work was not finished; she must go back. Each time, after climbing down only two steps, Mom awakened to numbing cold limbs and difficulty breathing.

The morning that followed Mom's third dream, she decided to tell the doctor about them. "Dr. Davis, I don't know if you believe in God or not, but for the last three nights I've dreamed that I went to heaven, but the Lord wouldn't let me in yet."

He responded in a solemn voice, "Well, young lady, we haven't known if we were going to keep you or lose you, but last night you finally passed the crisis!

From that day on Mom needed only to heal and regain her strength. She was finally released after spending sisteen days in the hospital.

My mother's dream of seeing Jesus and being in His presence for those brief moments filled her with a desire to obey and please Jesus for the rest of her days on earth.

Decades later, it has also become evident that the children in my mother's dream held an important significance. The vast majority of my mom's life has involved working with children. In addition to running a daycare, my parents took in over sixty foster children who lived with us for various periods of time. These kids referred to my mom as "Aunt Dolly."

One of the foster children that stands out in my memory was little Peggy Jane. Just four years old, she was blind, had cerebral palsy and wore heavy, steel braces on her frail legs. Her hips had been broken and reset to correct a birth defect and avoid a future walking disability.

Twice every day Mom would get down on her hands and knees, take Peggy's heavy braces off and massage her sore, thin legs. All the while Peggy would have her arms stretched up, wrapped around my mother's neck, exuberantly saying over and over, "I love you, Aunt Dolly!"

Often mom would hold Peggy on her lap and sing to her. Mom always sensed when children needed extra love and would take the time to give it to them.

Mom's greatest joy in life has always been to lead children to the Lord and to help them in their spiritual growth in any way she can. God has given her a special gift to teach children. For more than 65 years, Mom has taught Sunday school for various age groups. For numerous years she taught Junior Church at the Christian and Missionary Alliance Church in North Fort Myers, Florida.

At age 85, Mom admits she is slowing down and now only teaches Junior Church when a fill-in teacher is needed. She still senses when a child is feeling down or discouraged and makes a point to spend some time talking or praying with them whenever the opportunity presents itself.

Mom has never doubted that God sent her back to this life, with all its challenges, to minister to children.

One day my mother will again stand outside that gate, longing to go in. But the next time Jesus comes to meet her, He will say, "Well done, good and faithful servant! ... Come and share your Master's happiness!" (Matthew 25:21)

—Nina Stellwagen, Michigan

TAP ON THE SHOULDER

My Grandmother Sophie was just nineteen when her mother Elizabeth was in the final stage of a terminal illness. Sophie, being the only girl with five brothers, was extremely close to her mother and had been her chief caretaker for the past two years, since the beginning of her illness.

Elizabeth was a devout follower of Christ, which comforted Sophie, knowing her mother would go to be with the Lord when she passed on. Nevertheless, Sophie knew of the tremendous responsibility that would be placed on her shoulders caring for her brothers, who were often a difficult brood to handle. Sophie had already taken over doing the cooking and laundry for her father and brothers and was responsible for the rest of the household chores. She also took in ironing to help with the family finances. The prospective future was a burden that weighed heavily on her heart.

Elizabeth's days were drawing short, and Sophie began spending the nights sitting in a chair by her mother's bedside.

One night, exhausted, Sophie fell asleep in the chair. At approximately 1:10 a.m., she felt a tap on her shoulder and immediately became aware of a heavenly presence. The room was filled with a warm beautiful radiance. Then a comforting audible voice spoke to her, saying, "Don't be afraid. I'm here to take her. Everything is going to be fine." Sophie watched as her mother took her final breath, then the presence left the room.

My grandmother never doubted that she had been visited by an angel. She was greatly consoled and felt a total peace that everything was going to be OK. The heavenly visit provided her with strength to face the days and years ahead.

Later, Sophie married and had nine children of her own (my mother being one of them). Sophie's husband (my grandfather) eventually became an invalid.

My grandmother always felt that the years of caring for her mother and brothers prepared her to care for her own large family and physically disabled husband. The angel's visit brought my grandmother encouragement and comfort throughout her life.

"When I said, 'My foot is slipping,' Your love, O Lord, supported me. When anxiety was great within me, Your consolation brought joy to my soul."

- Psalm 94:18-19

—Nina Stellwagen, Michigan

GLIMPSE OF HEAVEN

Monday, March 26, 2007 started out like any ordinary day. I intended to accomplish several projects. The first task was to put a board along the edge of the driveway where the tulips that my wife Kay and I had planted would be coming up. Our hope was to keep our playful kittens from being able to get at the flowers.

In my workroom in our basement, I marked the board I intended to cut. Then I decided to take the board out to the garage to saw it, so as not to awaken one of our grown daughters who was staying with us and was still sleeping. Apparently, I was near the top of the basement stairway, when I fell backwards and landed headfirst on the floor below. My family later found my hammer at the top of the staircase and the board midway down the stairs.

On the basement floor, my body lay in a bloody mess. My skull was fractured, and I was bleeding from my ears, nose and mouth. My jaw was broken, as well as my nose, collarbone, tailbone and inner ear bone. My left shoulder was severely dislocated, and my left knee was badly injured. An ambulance took me to our local hospital, Central Michigan Community Hospital in Mt. Pleasant. From there I was transferred by helicopter to Covenant Healthcare in Saginaw.

At Covenant, a CAT scan revealed that my brain was swollen on both sides and bleeding. My right leg had several blood clots. The doctors gave me no chance of surviving. They told my wife I would be dead before the day was over and to call in the relatives. Being in a coma, I remembered none of this.

My last conscious memory was holding the board in my hand. The next moment I looked up and the Lord was standing right in front of me! He did not have to tell me who He was; I knew instantly. Since I've been walking and talking with Jesus since 1957, there was no need for an introduction. The board in my hand had disappeared, and Jesus and I started to walk together. "Yea, though I walk through the valley of the shadow of death, I will fear no evil; For You are with me ... " (Psalm 23:4, NKJV)

Ahead, I could see an enormous amount of light. It seemed as though Jesus and I just moved into it. To my astonishment, we began walking on a magnificent street of pure transparent gold. I remember looking down into it. Soft, glowing light emanated from the street. It was absolutely gorgeous. The Lord and I strolled along. To be in His presence was glorious—nothing else seemed to matter.

Jesus and I talked back and forth about numerous topics, yet now all I can recall is a single conversation. Jesus had asked me if there was anything I wanted to know or would like to see. Without hesitation, I told Him I wanted to see Calvary [the hill near Jerusalem where Jesus was crucified]. All my life as a minister, I had preached on Calvary and Christ crucified. No topic was dearer to my heart.

Suddenly, we were back 2,000 years in time, and I witnessed the crucifixion with the risen Lord standing at my side! The experience was beyond human comprehension. No words can adequately describe what I felt during that time. (Later, back on earth, the visual part of Christ's crucifixion was erased from my memory, but the beauty of what He had accomplished on the cross remained in my heart. For everyone that enters heaven, Calvary will be the reason we are there! Without Jesus taking the punishment for our sin, we would all be lost. "But God demonstrates his own love for us in this: While we were still sinners, Christ died for us." Romans 5:8)

Once again, Jesus and I were walking on the luminous street of gold. On both sides of the street, a grassy lawn area blanketed the ground. Some beautifully adorned mansions caught my eye. Although I could not tell what they were made of, the exteriors of all of them were white. What gave them color were jewels arranged in beautiful patterns, inlaid into the walls of these structures.

These were rare jewels of the universe that the Architect of the ages had created and placed there! The incredible light that filled heaven's atmosphere illuminated the jewels, creating stunning color and beauty. These heavenly abodes were completely furnished with elegant furniture. Everything was inexpressibly beautiful. Unlike earthly homes, I noticed that none of these dwellings had bedrooms or bathrooms. Neither is necessary in heaven!

One particular mansion that stood out to me had a diamond the size of a basketball imbedded into the side of it. Protruding out about six inches from the wall, the diamond had a striking brilliance. Peering into it, I observed there was not a single flaw that could be found. I marveled at its perfection. Its beauty was indescribable!

Somehow, it seemed as though this dwelling was to be my place of residence. No one in heaven told me that it was and maybe I'm wrong. But it was the only mansion that I had a clear memory of fixed in my mind after returning to my earthly life. I can picture it now as if I had seen it yesterday. Perhaps the diamond was there because, as a pastor, I have married numerous couples through the years. Nearly every bride-to-be has proudly shown me her diamond engagement ring.

Although everything in heaven was astonishing, it felt completely natural to be there. As on earth, there was constant activity. People were going places, doing things and visiting with one another. While in heaven, I saw my mother and Uncle Charlie. My mother was 84 when she died, but now appeared to be in her 30s. To see her again seemed as normal as coming into the house from playing when I was a kid and seeing her standing in the kitchen. My Uncle Charlie, who I was named after, was 79 when he died. Now he also appeared to be in his 30s. I saw the elderly people from the church I went to as a child. No one appeared to be old. Every person looked wonderful. Everyone was filled with joy.

The saints of all the ages were there, but I did not need to be introduced to anyone—they knew me and I knew them. I noticed that people were not exalted in any way—the Lord Jesus was the theme of heaven, and He alone was worshipped there!

In heaven there was no sense of time passing. If I died and went back right now, I honestly do not believe anyone would realize I had ever left—it would seem to everyone as though they had just seen me.

On earth, we commonly estimate time and distances, calculating approximately how much time it will take us to get from point A to point B. However, in heaven, with time removed, lengthy travel time was nonexistent. Often times, if I wanted to see someone or go somewhere, I would simply find myself there. The things that rule life on earth did not exist in heaven. What was truly amazing is that I did not seem surprised by any of this. At the time, everything I was experiencing felt completely ordinary—as though I had always been living in that marvelous place!

Clothed in my heavenly body, I felt exuberant, young, in superb health and perfect in every way. There was no fatigue or pain; no need or desire to sleep; no such thing as a dreary or sad thought. In heaven, our way of thinking was transformed. Emotions such as fear, anxiety or sorrow did not exist. While there, I had no idea that such emotions ever existed. Everything and everywhere in that Beloved City was joy and gladness. Every detail was planned and designed by the Lord. I was finally home.

All at once, I was back in "the valley of the shadow of death." Moments later, I found myself above a building looking down through a tile ceiling where I saw my severely injured body lying on a hospital bed. The thought entered my mind, "That's what this is all about!" Every fiber of my being wanted to stay with the Lord, but He made it clear that there was still a mission for me to accomplish here. I've never said "No" to Him before. Suddenly, I was back in my body.

For two weeks, I had been in a coma, totally oblivious to life on earth. Now I had no idea where I was. I remember thinking that I wanted to get off that bed, so that I could figure out where I was and go home.

When I attempted to get up, I discovered that I could not move my arms and legs. The nurses had me lying on my side with my good ear downward and my injured ear facing upward, so I could not hear. Because of my broken jaw, I could not call out to anyone. Also, everything was dark and I was unable to see. (Later I learned that my eyes had frozen open while I was in the coma. A heavy salve was put in my eyes to keep them from drying out).

There I was—unable to see, hear, talk, walk or move—and stuck in a body racked with pain. All I could do was lie there. Feeling like the ancient Bible character Job, I remember thinking, *I've got everything wrong, but leprosy!*

It took the staff a day and a half to realize I was coming out of my coma. I was transferred to a rehabilitation facility in Bay City to relearn how to walk and talk. Within a few weeks I was back home. Now, a few years later, I'm walking and getting around on my own, although not pain-free. Every time I visit my doctor, he says, "You know it's a miracle that you're alive, don't you!"

The Lord sent me back—not because I wanted to come back, but because He still had work for me to do. Everywhere I go, wherever they are willing to listen, I tell people my story.

Recently, I was in a large department store when one of the stock boys said to me, "Nice day."

I said, "Oh, it's a beautiful day! This is a day that the Lord has made, and we can rejoice in it!" He looked at me, stopped what he was doing, and I started telling him about my accident and time spent in heaven. He listened intently. At a later time, I went back to the store and looked the young man up. He had given his heart to the Lord, and it had changed his whole life. Such encounters have happened to me more times than I can remember. But if that young man was the only reason I was sent back, it was worth it!

Being given a glimpse of heaven has left me with an increased desire to tell others about Jesus and a great anticipation about living in my eternal home.

Everything on earth is temporary and full of decay. In heaven, there is no death or decay, sin, darkness, pain, tears or sorrow. It is the place where the King of Kings who rules the universe dwells, where everything is perfect and placed there by the God of all the ages. Heaven is eternal enjoyment and pleasure in the presence of the Lord!

"You will show me the path of life: in Your presence is fullness of joy; at Your right hand are pleasures for evermore."
- Psalms 16:11, NKJV

—Charles Booth, Michigan

THE ODOMETER

For many years I drove a bus, transporting special-needs adults and children. One cold February morning in 1996, I was on my daily run and had just entered the small town of Breckenridge, Michigan to pick up my first passenger.

Suddenly my thoughts were interrupted by a booming inner voice that clearly said, "Look at your mileage!"

The voice startled me. Even though it was not an audible voice, it was urgent and pressing. I knew it was God speaking to me and felt compelled to obey Him.

To read the odometer would not be a simple task. It was still dark outside, and the odometer on that particular bus was set into a control panel with poor lighting, and unusually small numbers. I would have to pull the bus over somewhere.

Before picking up my first client, I found the perfect opportunity to pull over. Quickly, I grabbed my glasses and a flashlight to help me see the odometer's row of little, individual wheels with numbers on each of them.

When I switched on the flashlight to reveal the mileage, the number illuminated was about to roll over. Cut precisely in half, I could see the bottom half of the number 6999.9 and, directly beneath it was the top half of the number 7000.0. At that very moment, the presence of the Lord swept over me, and God clearly spoke to me again, saying, "That's what time it is on My calendar!"

God put a keen understanding in me of what the numbers represented. The 6999.9 meant we were rapidly approaching the close of this age and that our time on Earth as we know it now is getting short! The 7000.0 represented Jesus' return to Earth to begin His thousand year reign over the nations. Following this golden age is the great white throne judgment (Revelation 20). Then the ultimate hope of everyone who puts his or her trust in Jesus is described in Revelation 21:1-4:

Then I saw a new heaven and a new earth, for the first heaven and the first earth had passed away, and there was no longer any sea. I saw the Holy City, the New Jerusalem, coming down out of heaven from God, prepared as a bride beautifully dressed for her husband. And I heard a loud voice from the throne saying, "Now the dwelling of God is with men, and He will live with them. They will be His people, and God Himself will be with them and be their God. He will wipe every tear from their eyes. There will be no more death or mourning or crying or pain, for the old order of things has passed away.

This incredible occurrence put a greater urgency within me that I needed to seek and follow the Lord with all my heart—and to serve Him while the opportunity exists!

". . . if you confess with your mouth, "Jesus is Lord," and believe in your heart that God raised Him from the dead, you will be saved."

-Romans 10:9

"Behold, I am coming soon! My reward is with Me, and I will give to everyone according to what he has done."

- Revelation 22:12

—Nina Stellwagen, Michigan

WOW of the *WOW Stories*

In 2005, soon after the Wow Stories venture began—when God so miraculously answered the prayer request concerning the first story in this book, Fly Away Checks—I realized then—this was God's project! He planned this long before the idea of writing a book revealing His love and power entered my mind! I was just one of the instruments used to bring His plan to pass. Time and again, God has confirmed His hand was on this book.

At the onset of the *Wow Stories* project, one hundred letters that included a bulletin insert were sent to churches in the surrounding areas, inviting people to share their WOW story for the upcoming book. Not one single person responded! To be honest, I became discouraged, but soon learned something. Every time I found myself backed up to a wall with inadequacies and frustrations, I would call out to God, asking Him to do what I was incapable of doing. He would always respond in a way that super-exceeded my expectations!

After my disappointment from the lack of response to the letters, nearly everywhere I went I would run into someone that had experienced a miracle or astonishing answer to prayer, or who had a relative or friend that did. Without any further effort on my part, God provided story after story!

Interesting things happened while writing the stories.

While working on the story Liver Transplant, and thinking about how incredible it was that precisely 365 days after Ken started his job, the very day his health insurance became activated to cover his preexisting liver disease he began hemorrhaging. If this had happened even one day before, Ken's medical expenses incurred that day and all future medical bills concerning his damaged liver would not have been covered by his health insurance, more than $2,000,000 worth!

I was typing away on his story thinking about how astounding God's timing is, when my computer crashed! It was around 9:30 on a

Saturday night. My husband Eric quickly retrieved our warranty from the file cabinet. We were shocked to discover the warranty expired the following day—the final day of a three-year contract! If the computer had crashed on my next work day, Monday, our policy would have been expired!

The Geek Squad was over within a few days and repaired the computer. I prayed diligently that nothing in the computer would be lost. We have a back-up system, but I had not remembered to download my work for quite some time. Thank the Lord—nothing was lost!

While writing certain stories, such as Memory Loss Gone and various healing accounts that revealed the power of using the authority of the name of Jesus and proclaiming His Word, I became aware of above average opposition going on in the spiritual realm. My head would begin to hurt, or I would have numerous irritating distractions, causing me to be tempted to turn off my computer. But, being quite sure where these assaults were coming from, I would simply command that all the enemy's tactics to keep me from writing, be canceled in the powerful name of Jesus. The Lord prevailed every time!

Once all the stories were written, I knew, because of my lack of professional writing skills, it would be important to have someone who was skilled in English carefully go over the stories.

I met with my friends (also prayer partners), MaryAnn Miiller and Claudia Wood, expressing my desire to find a college student with an English major to do a final edit of the Wow Stories book— someone who would be willing to take on this huge project without pay (at least for now).

MaryAnn, Claudia and I prayed diligently about the matter. Claudia made no mention that she was friends with a woman in Tennessee, who edited Christian books and did freelance writing for a living. A couple weeks later, on Thursday, March 4, 2010, I received an e-mail from Claudia:

Re: God Has Answered Your Prayer

Hi Nina!

Do you recall praying for an editor who has a college degree and experience? As you prayed, I knew that my friend, Diane Kilmer, was coming to town this week. She's an editor! She has her degree in English and edits books, newsletters, etc. for Christian writers for a living. I didn't want to mention it to you guys before talking to her, but she and I were talking last night and I mentioned that you'd finished your book and she said, "I'd really like to read that," so I asked her to think about editing it for you. She prayed about it and this morning said she'd be willing to look at it and see if she'd have time to right now.

I know you leave for Florida soon and I leave for Arizona tomorrow. Diane is speaking at a retreat today in Lansing, but will be back in town on Friday. You may either call me today, or e-mail Diane.

Have a great day!

Love in Christ, Claudia

Diane was still in Lansing when I received Claudia's e-mail. I contacted Diane and we set up a time to meet for the following day when she also planned to visit her son—who happened to live in the same small town as me!

So Friday afternoon I drove a mere 3 1/2 miles to a local restaurant and met with Diane! (My husband and I were scheduled to leave within hours for our annual trip to see my parents, four of my children and several grandkids who all live in southern Florida.)

I handed Diane the Wow Stories manuscript and Diane and I had a blessed short time, talking about the book and praying together.

After our praying, Diane told me that she felt led by the Lord to edit the book without charge! Diane also told me that she felt in her heart that the Lord would use the *Wow Stories* books as a tool in these last days to build people's faith and encourage them—the same message the Lord had been impressing on my heart! I was overjoyed!

I had planned to carefully review the book again while on vacation. What an added blessing to know I could just relax and enjoy the trip and visit with my family!

One month later, God did another amazing thing. On April 5, 2010, the day after Easter, I awoke at dawn from a vivid dream that I had the overwhelming sense was from God. The dream filled me with much happiness:

I was sitting alone in front of a massive wall and was quite pregnant! All at once, a large stack of receiving blankets in a variety of pastel colors, very neatly folded, appeared in my hands. I looked over to my right and realized I was either in a large church or auditorium. The room was filled with people sitting in chairs. A woman in the auditorium turned her head toward me and smiled. Her smile was huge and radiant. I was immediately aware that this woman had given me the receiving blankets and everything else I would need for my upcoming birth.

Because we were in some type of reverent atmosphere, all I could do was smile back at the woman. I mouthed the words "Thank you" to her. In the dream I was filled with gratitude beyond measure! Then I woke up. Instantly, the meaning of the dream flooded into my mind.

The Lord impressed on me that my life was in for major changes. Something new and wonderful was about to be birthed. My career as a writer was about to be launched, and new doors were about to be opened. The receiving blankets represented that every need I had would be met. There was a knowing imparted to me that I truly didn't need to spend so much as a moment concerning myself who the publisher of the Wow Stories book would be, or how I would come up with the necessary money that all the facets of publishing a book would cost. In fact, it was made perfectly known to me that every need for my future ministry would be taken care of by my Heavenly Father!

Elated emotions swept over me! What a happy, wonderful dream it was, removing every speck of future concerns about upcoming needed provisions!

Two days later, still basking in happiness, I told the dream to my son Scott over the phone. I was about to tell him what I felt impressed that the dream meant, when he abruptly interrupted me and said, "Don't say another word! God is giving me the interpretation of your dream to confirm to you that the dream was from Him and the meaning of the dream is true!"

Then Scott began, "That you were quite pregnant means you are on the verge and about to be launched into new ministry. Major changes are going to take place in your life. You are going to minister the love of God to others as never before!

"All kinds of changes are about to take place. The stack of receiving blankets that suddenly appeared in your hands means that every need you have will be met. You do not need to concern yourself with a single thing.

"The people in the building and the woman smiling at you represent that God will supply all your needs through the body of Christ. He will place it in their hearts to supply you with all your needs.

"The various shades of blankets mean the provisions will come from various people and places. That the stack of blankets suddenly appeared in your hands means God is going to suddenly shock you, meeting all your needs, just as He shocked you when He suddenly provided an editor for the Wow Stories book that totally surpassed your expectations!

"You don't need to worry about the publisher, money, etc. God will provide it all! You'll be amazed and shocked as you see Him provide all your needs for future ministry. You'll know beyond doubt God is doing this."

Since that dream, marvelous things have happened. One day I needed $20 to fill two ink cartridges so I could print out a hard copy of the *Wow Stories* book. I was in a grocery store and only had enough money to pick up a few necessary groceries, when I ran into one of my brother Dan's old friends. I began telling Glen about the *Wow Stories* book, when he pulled out a $20 bill and told me he felt led of the Lord to give it to me—seed faith toward expenses for the book. Twenty dollars was exactly what I needed that day!

Sometime later, I received a check in the mail for $150.00. A note enclosed explained the sender felt led of the Lord to send me seed-faith money for the *Wow Stories* book. The same week two other women felt led by God to give $50.00 each for *Wow Stories* book expenses! The Lord is manifesting the dream! Every expense I've incurred thus far has been met! Glory to God in the highest!

I recently received a check in the mail for $1,000 dollars from a woman I have never met or heard of! An enclosed note said she was having lunch with Diane (the editor) who told her about the book I was writing. God spoke to the woman, putting it in her heart to send $1,000 towards the *Wow Stories* book project. I was astounded again by God's provision and perfect timing! I would soon need money to pay Christina, the woman doing the *Wow Stories* book layout, as well as some other upcoming costs. Yippee God—my wonderful provider!

One day, a man who loves and follows the Lord diligently, began praying for the *Wow Stories* book. Before long, he saw a vision of Jesus looking through the Wow Stories book and stamping each page. He then proclaimed, "Jesus is putting His stamp of approval on every page!"

Using my human logic, I decided to submit the Wow Stories book to a Christian book publishing company. The application allowed me to give a 3,000-word sample of my writing. I decided to send four complete stories. Desiring the word count for the four stories to come as close to 3,000 as possible, I devised a plan.

After making a list of all the stories to be in the book, I wrote down the individual word count next to each of the stories. I would add up the numbers of three selected stories, and then subtract that total from 3,000. Then, I would scan the list for a story with a word count that would bring the total as near as possible to the 3,000-word limit without going over.

In the beginning of this process, I always selected stories I thought should be in the sampling. Every combination of stories I added up either went over 3,000 words, or substantially under what I was hoping for. After doing this over and over, I became frustrated and quit trying.

A couple days later, I decided to try again. But this time I prayed about it, saying something to the effect of, "Lord, You know four stories that would add up to precisely 3,000 words. Would You please do that for me?" So without hesitation or thought, I quickly checked off a new combination of three stories. On the very first attempt following prayer, there was a fourth story that brought the total word count to 2,999!

I burst out laughing and said, "All right, Abba Daddy Papa Father—You're being funny! There is no way that the God of the universe is going to be just one word off!" I felt as though God was being a fun-loving Father teasing His daughter. Immediately, without taking time or thought, I checked off another combination of three stories—and sure enough, there was a fourth story that brought the total word count to precisely 3,000! My Heavenly Father never ceases to amaze me!

A day or so later my sister Marie came over to visit. I was still excited about what God had done concerning the 3,000 word count, and told her all about it. During our conversation, it occurred to me that I had not paid any attention to what the four stories were.

Hurrying into our home office, I retrieved the list of stories. I had drawn matching symbols per four stories to keep track of all the combinations I had tried. Scanning the list for the four final stories that added up to 3,000, I was astonished to discover that the first story was one of mine, the second from my mother, the third another of mine, and the final story from one of my daughters! Quite remarkable when you consider there are dozens of stories from others in the book. I clearly knew that the four mom-daughter stories were no better or more exciting than any others in the book. This was just another of God's personal confirmations, showing His hand was on the *Wow Stories* book!

During the six months that the *Wow Stories* book was submitted online to be reviewed for prospective publishing, there was not a single response! However, during that time God put it in my heart to write three of my healing testimonies. As a result, these stories; *Amazing Love, Multi-Purpose Miracle* and *Heavenly Back Surgery*—are now included in the *Wow Stories* book. I can only assume someone needed to hear those stories.

When it came time to design a cover for the *Wow Stories* book, I desired for the cover to look like something that I could not explain. Any attempted cover designs, my own included, left me feeling disappointed. I wanted the cover to make a WOW statement of its own, drawing people's attention to it, causing them to want to stop and find out what the book was about.

Near the end of March, 2012, I was flying home from Florida a day or two after attending my daughter Nicole's wedding. I had my camera in my purse and decided to take some pictures of the clouds. I had the camera aimed to take another picture when I saw a flash. Spontaneously, I pushed the button on my camera. The flash turned out to be a jet soaring cross-wise beneath the plane. I remember thinking, WOW!

At some point, I began desiring to have the cloud-jet picture incorporated onto the Wow Stories book cover. My niece Kim downloaded the picture on her computer and started doing some experimenting. When she centered the jet in the middle of the WOW, I knew instantly that was it—what I'd been dreaming of—even though I had not known what that dream was!

Later, pondering all this, I thought, *What are the odds that someone would be taking pictures of the clouds out their airplane window and happen to capture a jet soaring cross-wise beneath you, yet still above the clouds?* I concluded that capturing this unexpected scene on camera was another of God's divinely ordained moments!

Although I was awed by the cloud-jet scene, and felt assured that it was God's divine plan for the cover, I was still slightly disappointed about the color and contrast. My niece did a fabulous job designing the front cover, but her graphics program was limited and she could not enhance the depth and color of the sky without diminishing the whiteness of the clouds.

My son Scott had been after me for some time to contact a girl named Melody concerning the cover. I never did, even though Scott kept telling me he felt God was putting this in his heart. One day I e-mailed the cover of the Wow Stories book to Scott, who, without telling me, forwarded it to Melody. Within a couple days Melody e-mailed the cover of the book to me after she had done some experimenting. I was stunned! She was able to enhance the color, contrast and depth of the clouds in a way that captured the dream in my heart!

Having a website, I learned, was essential for promoting the Wow Stories book. Checking out options, I found a company with pre-designed layouts for websites available at an affordable price. The company purchased a website domain for me, but as it turned out, none of their designs seemed to suit the need. To have a website personally modified was costly. The lowest estimate I found was for $1,000 dollars.

One evening while talking on the phone with Melody about the book cover, I mentioned my dilemma concerning the company I initially intended would make the Wow Stories website. Melody said: "I just learned how to build a website in one of my college classes and I would be glad to make the website." So, for a fraction of the typical cost, Melody designed a beautiful Wow Stories website! God has faithfully provided for every need!

When the time was drawing near to submit the WOW STORIES book for publication, in one day's time I incurred some major setbacks that could prevent the book's submission. I spent hours on the computer trying to deal with these problems without success. A few minutes after 9:00 p.m., out of sheer frustration I turned off the computer and walked out of our home office. Human logic was dominating my thoughts, so it's no wonder that I was soon overcome with discouragement. Fighting back tears, I called a prayer warrior friend so we could pray about the matter. While describing the situation to Debby, the call-waiting beep sounded on my phone. I could see that it was my son Scott. I quickly told Debby that I would call her back.

Scott lives in Florida, and he and I had not chatted on the phone for over a month. I pushed the call-waiting button and said "Hello!" Scott did not return my greeting, but in a bold, matter-of-fact tone blurted out: "Daughter! Do not be discouraged! I will fulfill everything I have promised you. Everything will come to pass!"

Afterward, Scott explained that he felt impressed by God to call me without delay. In obedience to God, Scott made the call—not having any idea of what he was going to say. Scott said the moment I said "Hello," the message from God poured into his mind, and then spontaneously flowed out of his mouth to me! Needless to say, all my discouragement instantly melted away and my sadness turned to joy and laughter. Within a couple days my predicaments were all solved as well! I will forever marvel that the Creator of the universe demonstrates His personal care over the smallest aspects of our lives!

In 2005, I never dreamed that eight years filled with numerous challenges, yet astounding answers to prayer, would pass by until it was God's perfect timing for the Wow Stories book to be published.

God has answered every prayer request, provided for every need, and taken care of every detail concerning the Wow Stories book in a manner that has surpassed all my expectations! I get excited just thinking about the miracles and astounding answers to prayers that are happening around the world that will one day fill future volumes of Wow Stories books!

All I can say is, "WOW!"

—Nina Stellwagen

Do You Have a WOW Story?

Job 5:9 declares, *He performs wonders that cannot be fathomed, miracles that cannot be counted.*

There is no doubt all of us would be astounded if we were to know how many miracles God performs around the world every single day!

If you have experienced a miracle from God, or an astonishing answer to prayer—we would love to hear your story.

You may e-mail your story to:

Hiswowstories@gmail.com.
Please type WOW STORY in the subject box.

Or, you may submit your story on the WOW STORIES website:

WWW.HISWOWSTORIES.COM

You will be notified if we plan to use your story in a future WOW STORIES book. We will be praying for God's direction and discernment on deciding which stories to include in future volumes.

Thank you!

ABOUT THE AUTHOR

Nina resides with her husband Eric in Michigan. They are now empty nesters, but cherish and enjoy any time spent with the kids, grandchildren, and greatgrandchildren.

In 1972, at age 21, Nina made Jesus her dearest, closest friend, which revolutionized her life!

For over three decades now, Nina's favorite pastime has been studying her Bible. Some of her favorite subjects are: the amazing love of God, Bible prophecy, victorious Christian living and great faith.

Throughout the years, she has taught numerous Bible studies and Sunday school classes, and has been a guest speaker at various women's ministry meetings. Nina also enjoys bringing hope and encouragement to young women finding themselves in difficult circumstances, and has been a volunteer peer counselor for Central Michigan Pregnancy Services for several years.

In 2004, Nina retired from her job with the goal of fulfilling her long-time dream of writing books.

In 2005, while writing a book on overcoming the emotional challenges that prevent weight loss, Nina suddenly had an immense desire to write a book filled with God's miracles and astounding answers to prayer. The weight-loss book was put on hold and Nina's efforts and focus were shifted to collecting and writing Wow Stories. She has no doubt this was God's divinely inspired project and the stories will bless, encourage and bring hope to many in the years to come.

Once the *Wow Stories* project is under way, Lord willing, Nina plans to complete the weight-loss book, to be followed by other books. She hopes to write on various topics that will aid followers of Christ in being overcomers in a world that evokes numerous spiritual battles and challenges.

Nina's greatest desire is to accomplish the work God has planned for her to do while living in this life.

Made in the USA
Charleston, SC
05 November 2013